RANGERS

OFFICIAL YEARBOOK 1999-2000

SIMPLY THE BEST

RANGERS WON IT ALL IN THE 1998-99 SEASON

The Scottish Premier League.

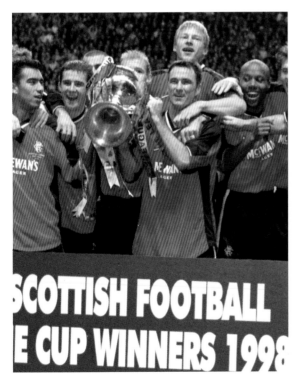

The Scottish League Cup.

The Scottish Cup.

RANGERS

OFFICIAL YEARBOOK 1999-2000

Paul Sinclair

Contributors/Acknowledgements

**NICKY PARIS, PAUL GEDDES, CRAIG STEVENS, JULIAN FLANDERS,
ROLAND HALL, NICK PEEL, GILLIAN PLATT, ALASTAIR GOURLAY
THANKS ALSO TO ALL THE CLUBS WHO KINDLY GRANTED PERMISSION IN ALLOWING
THEIR OFFICIAL CLUB CRESTS TO BE REPRODUCED IN THIS PUBLICATION**

Photographs

**DEREK STEWART AND ALAN WHYTE AT RANGERS FOOTBALL CLUB
ACTION IMAGES
THE DAILY RECORD**

First published in 1999 by

RANGERS BOOKS

an imprint of

ANDRE DEUTSCH LTD

76 DEAN STREET

LONDON WIV 5HA

www.vci.co.uk

Published by André Deutsch Ltd under licence from

THE RANGERS FOOTBALL CLUB

IBROX STADIUM

GLASGOW G51 2XD

Design and editorial

DESIGN/SECTION, FROME

ISBN

0 233 99772 5

Printed and bound in the UK by

BUTLER & TANNER LIMITED, FROME AND LONDON

CONTENTS

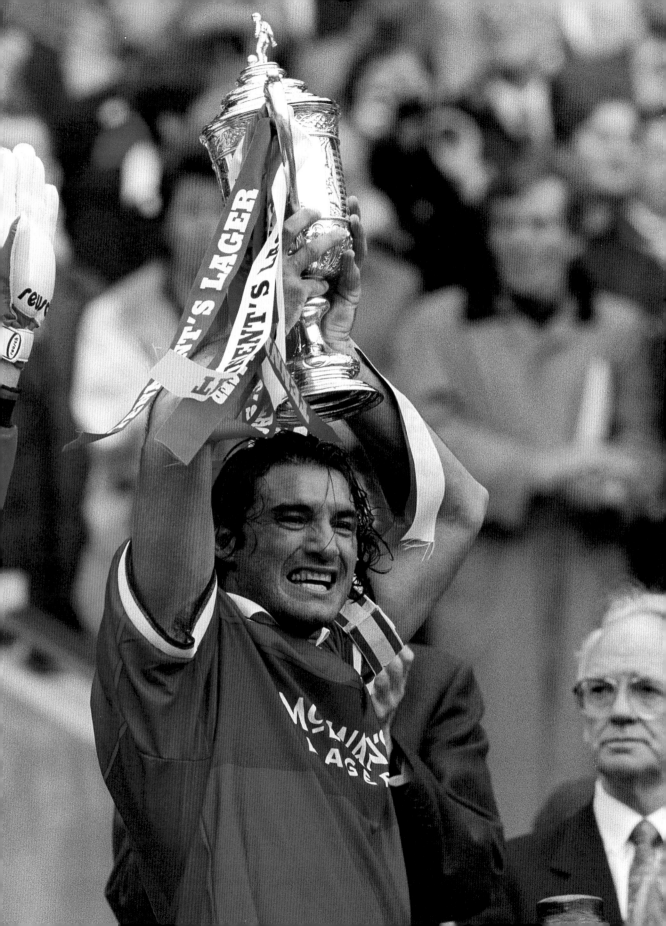

CHAIRMAN'S MESSAGE by David Murray

Last season was the beginning of a new era for Rangers, and a fabulously successful one at that. After the success of the Walter Smith years, we moved into a new style with Dick Advocaat, but the change of direction didn't mean we stopped winning. Rangers won more, recording a record sixth domestic treble. Dick has re-built almost an entire squad, and deserves enormous credit for being able to do that in just one season and to keep winning while it was done. He has the basis on which to build even more success in the future.

But Dick's approach has been to build a squad of players who can all do their part rather than rely on the skills of one or two individuals. It has brought rewards. That squad will be strengthened as and when Dick feels it is necessary, but in this new era there is also a greater emphasis on youth.

The way forward for all clubs throughout Europe is to bring on their own young talent, rather than to rely on the increasingly inflated transfer market. We have seen the success of our youth policy in the emergence of young Barry Ferguson, and there will be more coming through the ranks in years to come. There must be a balance in buying in fresh talent and developing our own.

Dick, and his assistant Bert Van Lingen, haven't just been working on the first team, they have brought a new approach to the entire club and that will bear more fruit in the years to come. We are now better prepared to compete in Europe and take on the challenges of the future.

Every Rangers supporter will have seen the changes, and enjoyed the success. But one thing hasn't changed and never will – the importance of the fans. Without you, the Rangers supporters, neither Dick nor I would have been able to build what we have. We can look forward to a tremendous future together.

— *David E. Murray*

MANAGER'S MESSAGE by Dick Advocaat

Last season's performance from the first-team squad was the result of a great deal of hard work.

When I took over as manager, Rangers needed almost a completely new team and building a new side always takes time. The fact that we went on to win every domestic honour last season shows just how hard the players worked and how well they responded.

One of the strange things about Scottish football is how easily those within it put it down, but I maintain that the football in the Scottish Premier League is of a high quality. There are no easy fixtures in the top ten.

Now that we have the foundations of the squad in place, this season we hope to build on what was achieved last time, although repeating the treble is not going to be easy!

What I hope is that the players can develop further as a team, and that we can heighten the quality of our performances as well as maintaining the consistency of last term.

There was no big spending in the summer because there did not need to be. I will always be looking to add quality players to the squad, but now that we are settled we can look forward to this squad of players achieving even more over the next couple of seasons than they did last term.

— Dick Advocaat

THE ADVOCAAT REVOLUTION

When Dick Advocaat took over from Walter Smith, Rangers FC were not only welcoming a new manager, they were entering a new era. Out with Smith went almost an entire team. In with Advocaat came nearly a whole squad's worth of new players – and a new method.

Smith had been remarkably successful as both manager, and before, as assistant to Graeme Souness, when Rangers dominated Scottish football for more than a decade – winning ten League Championships in 11 years and a host of Scottish and League Cups. Smith had delivered the coveted nine successive titles and had equalled Celtic's prized record. But real success in Europe had eluded him, and in a disappointing final season, Rangers' ageing team, hampered by a succession of injuries, could neither claim the elusive tenth successive title, nor any trophy at all. When Advocaat came in there was work to be done but in some ways after a 'bare' season the pressure could have been off him – he had no run to keep going. But in another sense it was more intense: Rangers supporters don't expect to finish any season without a trophy – let alone two in a row.

Advocaat had to change a squad – a mentality – and had to win the Championship in his first season while he was at it, to be seen as a success. He passed some Ibrox legends on the way through the door. Ex-captain Richard Gough had been asked back to help out Smith in his hour of need at Everton – and left at the same time. Ally McCoist and Ian Durrant both

Rich Reward: the Ibrox crowd were given a great treat at the end of the season – an FA Cup win over Celtic.

left to finish their careers at Kilmarnock. Stuart McCall, the engine in midfield for so many years, said a tearful farewell, while for 'the Goalie', Andy Goram, leaving Ibrox was worse than leaving home. Others, like Joachim Bjorklund, Alex Cleland and Peter van Vossen, parted on less emotional terms.

And before Advocaat even got to Ibrox, two players who had been Rangers' inspiration in Smith's later years – Paul Gascoigne and Brian Laudrup – had moved on to the English Premiership. The departure of those last two players in particular saw a change in style under Advocaat. As he assembled his new squad, there was to be no place for any one outrageous talent for the team to depend on. With Advocaat there was to be a system, flexible at times and fluid, but a method of playing thoughtful, passing football in which everyone would play a part.

Class Act: Dutch international Giovanni van Bronckhorst, signed fresh from the 1998 World Cup, won over the crowd with his stunning free-kicks and deft control.

Backed by Rangers chairman David Murray, the new management team spent almost £27 million on assembling a new squad. At the back they bought French international goalkeeper Lionel Charbonnier for £1.2 million from Auxerre. In front of him came the Scotland captain Colin Hendry for £4 million from Blackburn, and the luckless Daniel

The New Guard: Dick Advocaat and the men on his bench. It was a complete transformation from the previous season's management line-up.

Prodan, whose knee injury would keep him out for the season after his £2.2 million move from Atletico Madrid.

Then there were perhaps two of Advocaat's most significant signings, men he knew well from Holland. He went back to his old club, PSV Eindhoven, to buy Arthur Numan for £5 million. The Dutch international left-back had played for Advocaat at three other clubs before arriving at Ibrox. With him came another member of Holland's 1998 World Cup squad, Giovanni van Bronckhorst – bought from Feyenoord for £5.25 million. For a bit of panache on the wing, Advocaat went to Italy to buy Andrei Kanchelskis from Fiorentina for a club record, £5.5 million. In attack, he splashed out £4.2 million for Real Mallorca's Argentinian striker Gabriel Amato to partner Rod Wallace whom Advocaat shrewdly signed for no fee from Leeds United under freedom of contract.

As the new players became acquainted with their new surroundings, the players already at Ibrox came to terms with a new, more disciplined regime. Advocaat and his assistant Bert van Lingen quickly established a strong code of conduct which could not be deviated from by any player, however big their reputation. There were to be no favourites and no shirking, as the two tried to fashion their squad of individuals into a team.

A number of players already at Ibrox flourished under the new management. Barry Ferguson was almost a new player and went on to play a significant part in the season ahead, as did Jonatan Johansson in a new role as striker. Defenders like Craig Moore and Tony Vidmar, who were never highly regarded by the fans, were to win them over with their dynamic, much improved performances.

But despite the excitement of the Advocaat revolution, and the re-casting of the squad and the training methods, the new manager was well aware that neither he nor the fans would be satisfied if it didn't result in the Championship flag coming back across the city to Ibrox. Neither Advocaat nor Rangers were to be disappointed in a season which maintained its excitement right to the end.

Back In Britain: Andrei Kanchelskis, a former favourite at Manchester United and Everton, was tempted away from Italy and became Rangers' record signing.

1998-99

MATCH BY MATCH

THE FOLLOWING SECTION LISTS EVERY FIRST-TEAM COMPETITIVE GAME FROM THE 1998-99 SEASON.
IN THE TEAM LINE-UPS, PLEASE NOTE: SCORERS AND THEIR GOAL TIMES ARE MARKED IN RED, SUBSTITUTES ARE
LISTED IN BRACKETS WITH THE TIME THEY CAME ON AND TWO YELLOW CARDS INDICATE A SENDING-OFF.
ALSO, FOR SPL GAMES, TWO UNDER-21 PLAYERS SAT ON THE BENCH BUT HAVE NOT BEEN LISTED.

SHELBOURNE 3 5 RANGERS

match highlights

UEFA Cup 1st Qualifying Round
1st Leg 22 July 1998
Attendance: 6,047
Referee: V Anghelinei (Romania)

Before Dick Advocaat officially took over as manager, Rangers fans were warned they would have to get used to changes. But both Advocaat and Ibrox diehards were glad that one traditional quality was not swept away – Rangers would still fight to the last. In this game they found that they had to.

With 58 minutes gone it looked as though Rangers were facing their worst ever humiliation in Europe – they were 3-0 down to Irish part-timers Shelbourne. Comic cuts defending had given the Dublin club a 2-0 lead at half-time. After just seven minutes Sergio Porrini tried to head away a cross, but instead put the ball in his own net. Three minutes before the break Antti Niemi joined him in the doghouse. He flapped at a corner from the left, missed the ball and as it came back across goal Mark Rutherford drove it into the net.

Advocaat brought on Gabriel Amato and Jonatan Johansson for David Graham and Rino Gattuso, but before they made an impact Rangers were 3-0 down when Paul Morley scored 13 minutes after the restart. Rangers needed a break and got it immediately when an Amoruso header was handled in the box. Albertz took the penalty and Rangers were at last on the scoreboard.

What happened in the last 18 minutes was truly dramatic. First, Amato scored after a Petric shot had been kicked off the line. Two minutes later Rangers, remarkably, were level. Giovanni van Bronckhorst went on a run down the left before cracking home a drive from 15 yards. With eight minutes to go, a now-rampant Rangers took the lead when Amato headed in a Johansson cross from the left. Three minutes later Albertz scored with his second penalty after another handball, and an astonishing comeback was complete.

This match was moved from Dublin to Tranmere Rovers' ground in Birkenhead in an attempt to prevent crowd trouble. Unfortunately there was still fighting outside the ground, and Shelbourne keeper Gough was hit by a tin can.

Gabriel Amato heads in a Johansson cross to give Rangers the lead for the first time in the match.

SHELBOURNE

Gough
Geoghegan
McCartney
Scully
Baker
Rutherford 42
Smith
Fenlon
Fitzgerald
Morley 58 (Sheridan 78)
Kelly

substitutes
Campbell
Neville
Flood
Gifford
R Baker
O'Brien
Sheridan

RANGERS

Niemi
Porrini (og) 7
Amoruso
Petric
Van Bronckhorst 74
Gattuso (Amato 46)
B Ferguson
Thern (I Ferguson 63)
Albertz (2 pens) 59, 85
Graham (Johansson 46)
Durie

substitutes
Amato 72, 82
Charbonnier
I Ferguson
Johansson
Moore
Vidmar
Wilson

RANGERS 2　0 SHELBOURNE

UEFA Cup 1st Qualifying Round
2nd Leg 29 July 1998
Attendance: 46,906
Referee: M Milewski (Poland)

match highlights

Every Rangers player who was allowed to stay at the club after Dick Advocaat's appointment wanted to impress the new regime early on. At the start of the season no one was taking his opportunity better than Jonatan Johansson. He had come on as a substitute to help get Rangers out of jail in the first leg of this tie – now his two goals at Ibrox would confirm their place in the next round. Johansson's goal after four minutes was his first ever for the club. Manager Dick Advocaat had taken a risk on the fitness of Andrei Kanchelskis and Arthur Numan, probably to give them a run out before the League started the following weekend. Kanchelskis repaid his faith immediately with a marvellous cross from the right after just four minutes and Johansson clipped the ball home.

With the tie as good as won – with an aggregate score of 6-3 at the time – Rangers struggled to get a second and the match became something of a training exercise. Both Durie and van Bronckhorst saw efforts hit the crossbar, but the match lacked bite. Kanchelskis was kept in at half-time and was replaced by Amato, but the Argentinian didn't have the touch which had given him two goals the week before. The biggest cheer of the second half came when Advocaat rushed out of the dug-out and back-heeled the ball back into play for a free-kick to be taken.

The fans had to wait until the last minute of the match for Johansson's second goal. Numan supplied a cross from the left, and when substitute Rino Gattuso's shot was blocked, Johansson was lurking to drive the ball home from six yards.

RANGERS

Niemi
Porrini
Moore
Amoruso
Numan
Kanchelskis (Amato 45)
B Ferguson
Van Bronckhorst (I Ferguson 74)
Albertz
Durie (Gattuso 62)
Johansson 4, 89

substitutes
Amato
Brown
I Ferguson
Gattuso
Graham
Petric
Thern

SHELBOURNE

Gough
Geoghegan
McCartney
Scully
Baker
Rutherford
Smith
Fenlon
Fitzgerald
Morley (Sheridan 67)
Kelly

substitutes
Sheridan
O'Brien
Neville
Gifford
Byrne
R Baker
Campbell

Johansson scored at both ends of the match to see Rangers through to the next round.

HEARTS 2   1 RANGERS

match highlights

Scottish Premier League
1 August 1998
Attendance: 15,982
Referee: H Dallas (Motherwell)

Dick Advocaat started his first Scottish League campaign as his predecessor Walter Smith had ended his Rangers career – with a defeat by Hearts. The Edinburgh side had more than their share of luck against a makeshift Ibrox side. Injuries to four central defenders meant that Advocaat had to reshuffle his back four, moving Rino Gattuso to right-back and partnering Sergio Porrini with Craig Moore in the heart of the rearguard. Doubts over the fitness of Andrei Kanchelskis and Gabriel Amato saw them relegated to a place on the bench but both came on in a thunderous second half when Rangers – 2-1 down – were desperately unlucky not to equalise, let alone win the match.

The match started badly for the Glasgow side. After just five minutes Arthur Numan was unable to clear a cross from Neil McCann, and when the ball fell to Stephane Adam he poked it into the net from six yards. After 20 minutes Rangers were 2-0 down. The unfit-looking Jonas Thern was caught dithering just 25 yards from his own goal. Adam put in a tackle and the ball broke to Hearts' Jim Hamilton, who stepped away from Porrini and lashed the ball across goalkeeper Niemi and into the net. Rangers looked to be reeling but the sharp instincts of Rod Wallace saw them back in the game just eight minutes later. Gordon Durie set up Giovanni van Bronckhorst for a pop at goal, but when the Dutchman sliced his effort across the six-yard box, Wallace reacted first and drove the ball into the net.

In the second half, Advocaat went all out to save the match. He brought on Kanchelskis for Thern, and moved to a three-pronged attack. Both van Bronckhorst and Wallace were unlucky not to score, before he added to Rangers' firepower with the introduction of Amato for the Dutch midfielder. Rangers pounded shot after shot at the Hearts goal, but with Giles Rousset on top form they could find no way through.

HEARTS

Rousset
Naysmith
Weir
Salvatori
Ritchie
McCann
Fulton
Adam 6 (Murray 86)
Hamilton 20
Locke
Flogel

substitute
McKenzie
Quitongo
Holmes
Milne
Murray

RANGERS

Niemi
Porrini
Numan
Van Bronckhorst (Amato 65)
Durie
Albertz
Thern (Kanchelskis 46)
I Ferguson
Wallace 28
Gattuso
Moore

substitutes
Amato
Brown
Kanchelskis
Nicholson
Vidmar

Rod Wallace drives the ball into the net for Rangers' only goal of the match.

RANGERS 2 0 PAOK SALONIKA

UEFA Cup 2nd Qualifying Round
1st Leg 11 August 1998
Attendance: 35,392
Referee: K M Nielsen (Denmark)

RANGERS

Niemi
Porrini
Moore
Amoruso
Numan
Kanchelskis 55
B Ferguson (Albertz 67)
I Ferguson
Van Bronckhorst (Gattuso 78)
Wallace 68
Durie (Amato 6)

substitutes
Amato
Albertz
Charbonnier
Gattuso
Petric
Johansson
Miller

PAOK SALONIKA

Mihopoulos
Bantovic
Olivares
Kapetanopoulos
Vrizas (Cominges 66)
Toursounidis (Zafiriou 45)
Frantzeskos
Nagbe
Katisatis
Konstanpinibis
Macheridis

substitutes
Zafseiriou
Cominges
Koulakiotis
Balis
Argyriou
Merisaoies
Uafes

match highlights

If there was one area in which Dick Advocaat was expected to make Rangers perform, it was in Europe. After the scare against Shelbourne, this was his first test against 'respectable' opposition. Both he and his team passed it with flying colours. A mature display of patience and thoughtful passing football saw them overcome the physical Greeks and establish a commanding lead in the first leg. PAOK made their intentions clear very early in the game. First a 30-yard thunderbolt shot from Liberian Joe Nagbe flashed wide. Then after just three minutes Gordon Durie was taken out of play by a horrendous tackle from Macheridis. Durie took no further part in the game and was replaced by Amato, while the Greek was booked. Four minutes later and Macheridis was off, booked for the second time when he kicked the ball away at a free-kick.

Depite the early violence Rangers settled quickly. With Barry Ferguson pulling the strings in midfield, they carved out a number of chances in the first half, but couldn't get the break in front of goal. Wallace ran on to a beautiful through ball from Ferguson but couldn't find the net, and then Amato missed an easy header.

Jorg Albertz powers another shot towards the Salonika goal after coming on as a second-half substitute.

Rangers had to wait until the 55th minute to make the breakthrough. Wallace whipped in a dangerous cross from the left. Sergio Porrini shaped up for a header at the far post, but then wisely left it for the incoming Kanchelskis. He met the ball with a flying header and it bulleted into the net.

Advocaat brought on Jorg Albertz for the tiring Barry Ferguson and the German immediately set up the second goal. Albertz picked up the ball in midfield and galloped towards the Greek goal. He found Wallace with a short pass on the edge of the box and demanded the return for a one-two. But on a night when Rangers were taking all the right options, Wallace instead spun round and cracked a right foot shot hard into the net for Rangers' second – and some breathing space to take back to Greece.

RANGERS 2 1 MOTHERWELL

match highlights

Scottish Premier League
15 August 1998
Attendance: 49,275
Referee: G Simpson (Westhill)

Motherwell came to Ibrox to frustrate Rangers, and with the Ibrox side still trying to adapt to Dick Advocaat's new style, this was a victory which was ground out rather than achieved with any degree of flamboyance.

But it had looked as though Rangers would rip the Lanarkshire side apart when they took the lead after just 14 minutes with the best move of the match. Van Bronckhorst and Numan combined well on the left, and when the full-back whipped in a cross, Rod Wallace ghosted away from his marker and flighted a header past Steve Woods in the Motherwell goal. After that Rangers should have settled down, but they failed to find their rhythm.

With Colin Hendry making his Ibrox debut, the home side's rearguard didn't really settle.

Few clear-cut chances were made by either side as Motherwell tried to block Rangers' every move, and seven minutes after the break, the visitors grabbed a shock equaliser. Owen Coyle was released down the right, and although Hendry stepped out to play offside, Sergio Porrini played him on. Amoruso tried to play Coyle wide, but before the defender could get a tackle in, the Motherwell striker managed to squeeze a shot across Lionel Charbonnier and into the corner of the net.

In the last 20 minutes Rangers piled on the pressure to retrieve the lead. Albertz came close with a scorching free-kick and Hendry had a header cleared off the line.

With the match in injury time, Albertz swung in a corner from the left. In desperation, Motherwell defender Kai Nyyssonen for some reason handled the ball and Rangers were awarded a penalty. Albertz strode up and powered the ball into the net, and Rangers had won their first League points of the season – albeit against the odds.

Giovanni van Bronckhorst combined well with Arthur Numan to set up Rangers' first goal.

RANGERS

Charbonnier
Porrini
Amoruso
Numan
Kanchelskis
Van Bronckhorst
Amato (Graham 83)
Albertz (pen) 90
I Ferguson (Johansson 63)
Wallace 16
Hendry

substitutes
Gattuso
Graham
Johansson
Moore
Niemi

MOTHERWELL

Woods
McGowan
Valakari (McCulloch 45)
McClair
Coyle 52
Michels
Doesburg
Matthaei (Halliday 71)
Stirling
Teale
Nyyssonen

substitutes
Denham
Halliday
Kaven
McCulloch
White

RANGERS 4   0 ALLOA

Scottish League Cup 3rd Round
18 August 1998
Attendance: 37,201
Referee: J Rowbotham (Kirkaldy)

RANGERS

Charbonnier
Porrini
Amoruso 2
Numan
B Ferguson 42
Van Bronckhorst
Amato
Albertz 60, 82
Wallace (Miller 62)
Gattuso
Hendry (Moore 8)

substitutes
I Ferguson
Moore
Miller

ALLOA

Cairns
Valentine
Nelson
McAneny
McCulloch (Haddow 45)
Pew
Wilson
Ramsay (McKay 71)
Simpson
Irvine
McKechnie (Cameron 71)

substitutes
Cameron
Haddow
McKay

match highlights

The value of competing in the League Cup had already been doubted by Dick Advocaat – as it was by Walter Smith before him. With a crucial UEFA Cup tie looming, matches like this are not always welcome. With all due respect to Alloa, who fought for every minute, the match was an irritation that Rangers just wanted to get out of the way in the fixture-packed early weeks of the season.

Both sides of the argument were illustrated within the first few minutes. As a contest the match was virtually over after 90 seconds, when Lorenzo Amoruso headed a van Bronckhorst cross in off the underside of the bar. But the dangers of these games were seen six minutes later when new signing Colin Hendry had to limp off with an ankle injury. Not the kind of preparation you want for Europe. Rangers continued to press, but a lack of imagination against a packed Alloa defence meant that chances were restricted. It took them until the 42nd minute to add to their lead – with their first competitive goal of the season from a Scot. Wallace was the provider with a good run down the flank, and when he cut back, Barry Ferguson slammed the ball into the net with his left foot from 15 yards.

At its best this game was an exhibition match, and Jorg Albertz was to provide the finest exhibits. He made it 3-0 for the home side with a breathtaking free-kick from 25 yards, which the Alloa keeper might have heard, but he certainly didn't see. Eight minutes from time he did it again, this time bulleting in a shot from 20 yards high into the net.

Albertz turns to the crowd after scoring his second goal of the afternoon.

KILMARNOCK 1 3 RANGERS

match highlights

Scottish Premier League
22 August 1998
Attendance: 17,608
Referee: K Clark (Paisley)

Kilmarnock were early leaders in the Scottish Premier League and it was important for Rangers to stop their bandwagon before it really got going. Before half an hour had gone they had done exactly that. Kilmarnock manager Bobby Williamson tried to stop the threat of Arthur Numan's forward runs by playing Jerome Vareille on the right, but the midfield power from the on-song Barry Ferguson proved to be the inspiration the Ibrox side needed. It was Ferguson who created the first clear chance of the day when he found Rod Wallace with a beautifully weighted pass, but the Kilmarnock keeper Gordon Marshall stood up well.

When Rangers did break through, Wallace was both chance maker and chance taker. He put van Bronckhorst in the clear and when the midfielder's shot was parried by Marshall, Wallace scampered onto the rebound and tucked it away. Four minutes later and Rangers had a 2-0 lead. Again it was Ferguson who found Wallace with a delightful ball, but when the striker tried to turn in the box he was brought down by Kilmarnock centre-half Jim Lauchlan. It was a clear penalty, and Jorg Albertz scored from the spot.

The game looked over, but seven minutes into the second half, Rangers' early season defensive frailties gifted the home side a goal. Paul Wright found Vareille with a diagonal ball, and the Frenchman steamed into the Rangers penalty area. He was challenged by van Bronckhorst and when the ball broke to Lorenzo Amoruso – under pressure from Wright – the Rangers captain for some reason passed back to goalkeeper Lionel Charbonnier. Charbonnier could only chest the ball down and Wright nipped in to score.

The goal could have turned the match the home side's way, but their battling was undermined when Lauchlan was sent off for his second bookable offence – a late tackle on van Bronckhorst. There was no way back after that, and with four minutes to play Rangers sealed their victory. Marshall could only parry an effort from Wallace and substitute Charlie Miller slid in to score Rangers' third.

KILMARNOCK

Marshall
MacPherson
Kerr
McGowne
Holt
Wright 52
Durrant
Mitchell (Mahood 80)
McCoist (Nevin 88)
Vareille (Burke 78)
Lauchlan

substitutes
Baker
Burke
Mahood
Nevin

RANGERS

Charbonnier
Porrini
Amoruso
Numan
B Ferguson
Kanchelskis (Gattuso 80)
Van Bronckhorst
Amato (Miller 74)
Albertz 29 (pen)
Wallace 25
Moore

substitutes
Brown
I Ferguson
Gattuso
Petric
Miller 86

Rod Wallace turns to Andrei Kanchelskis in triumph having put Rangers ahead after 25 minutes.

PAOK SALONIKA 0   0 RANGERS

UEFA Cup 2nd Qualifying Round
2nd Leg 25 August 1998
Attendance: 32,000
Referee: M Merk (Germany)

PAOK SALONIKA

Mihopoulos
Bantovic
Olivares
Zafiriou (Uafes 72)
Kapetanopoulos
Frantzeskos
Vrizas (Cominges 52)
Toursounidis (Marifaliev 66)
Nagbe
Koulakiotis
Katisatis

substitutes
Argyriou
Uafes
Velis
Samaras
Marifaliev
Cominges
Mastos

RANGERS

Charbonnier
Porrini
Amoruso (Petric 77)
Numan
B Ferguson
Kanchelskis (Gattuso 81)
Van Bronckhorst
Albertz (Amato 61)
I Ferguson
Wallace
Moore

substitutes
Amato
Gattuso
Johansson
Miller
Niemi
Petric
Vidmar

match highlights

The Greeks have long since stopped bearing gifts of any sort – certainly on the football field. In fact they are not hospitable hosts at all. The Rangers players found that out when they turned up at the ground two hours before kick-off to be greeted by thousands of angry jeering fans. When you realise PAOK's ground is nicknamed 'the Tomb' and the fans call themselves collectively 'the Black Death' you get an idea of the atmosphere there.

But Rangers weren't giving anything away either. They survived an opening barrage from the Greek side, and when Olivares managed to break through after 12 minutes he found Charbonnier on fine form. After the initial onslaught, Rangers started to creep forward and when van Bronckhorst came close with a shot, PAOK seemed to take fright and restricted themselves to more cautious long-range efforts. The closest they came to scoring in the first half was when a free-kick came off van Bronckhorst but – with Charbonnier beaten – it span wide of the post.

With temperatures still in the 80s in the second half, PAOK threw themselves forward as Rangers began to tire. They had three good chances to score, but luck was on Rangers' side. First a shot from Cominges squeezed under Charbonnier, but he managed to stop it with his rear end. Then Toursounidis beat the keeper with a shot but Barry Ferguson was on the line to knock it clear.

The Greeks grew desperate by the end, and when Charbonnier was beaten again by a shot from Frantzeskos, you could taste their frustration as the ball came off the crossbar. It was Rangers' composure in difficult circumstances which restricted the Greeks to so few efforts – but the team were mightily relieved to hear the final whistle.

Glad It's Over: Arthur Numan and friends celebrate the end of a gruelling two-leg European tie.

RANGERS 4   0 ST JOHNSTONE

match highlights

Scottish Premier League
29 August 1998
Attendance: 48,732
Referee: H Dallas (Motherwell)

Of all Dick Advocaat's multi-million pound signings, the most impressive player in the Rangers squad in the early part of the season was one who had cost nothing and was already there when the Dutchman arrived – Barry Ferguson. Surprisingly left out of Craig Brown's squad for the Scotland match against Lithuania, Ferguson tried to prove the national manager had been wrong by dominating the game against St Johnstone and creating three of Rangers' four goals.

The first came after 25 minutes, when he found Andrei Kanchelskis on the right. His pass beat the offside trap and the Russian ran on and lobbed Alan Main in the Saints goal from 16 yards. Just before half-time, Ferguson's vision and imagination created a second. This time a perfectly-paced pass found van Bronckhorst, who cracked home a 20-yard shot to put the home side two up. St Johnstone's plan to come to Ibrox and frustrate Rangers had failed, and in the second half they tried to attack. Charbonnier made two excellent saves from Roddy Grant, but within ten minutes of the re-start Rangers were three up – and Ferguson was the orchestrator again.

The 20-year-old split the Saints defence with a through ball which Rod Wallace ran on to and the striker tucked the ball into the net from a tight angle for the third. Jorge Albertz completed the victory with a penalty five minutes from time, but by that time Barry Ferguson had gone off to a standing ovation to be replaced by his namesake Ian, knowing he had led his team to the top of the League.

*'Barry Ferguson is as **talented in his position** as Michael Owen is in his and he should be in the Scotland team to give him a taste for it'*

— ROD WALLACE

RANGERS

Charbonnier
Porrini
Amoruso
B Ferguson (I Ferguson 75)
Kanchelskis 26
Van Bronckhorst 45
Amato (Miller 66)
Albertz 85 (pen)
Wallace 56
Moore
Vidmar (Hendry 72)

substitutes
I Ferguson
Graham
Hendry
Miller

ST JOHNSTONE

Main
McQuillan
Preston (Bollan 69)
Scott
O'Neil
Grant
Kane
Griffin
O'Halloran (McMahon 67)
Dods
Simao (Lowndes 56)

substitutes
Bollan
Lowndes
McMahon
Whiteford

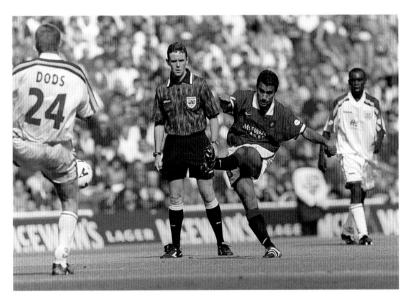

Giovanni van Bronckhorst blasts a shot into the St Johnstone goal and scores, just before half-time.

AYR UNITED 0 2 RANGERS

Scottish League Cup
Quarter-final 8 September 1998
Attendance: 11,198
Referee: M McCurry (Glasgow)

AYR UNITED

Nelson
Robertson
Miller
Millen
Welsh
Craig
Hurst
Davies
Walker (Ferguson 75)
Findlay
Lyons

substitutes
Ferguson
Kelly
Traynor

RANGERS

Charbonnier
Porrini
Moore (Hendry 50)
Amoruso
Vidmar
Johansson
B Ferguson
Van Bronckhorst
Wallace
Amato 13 (I Ferguson 86)
Albertz (Miller 46)

substitutes
I Ferguson
Hendry
Miller 85

match highlights

Rangers only showed the type of flowing football that Dick Advocaat is aiming to make their hallmark in flashes, but it was enough to beat a very well-organised Ayr United team and progress to the semi-finals of the League Cup.

The rain lashed down on Ayr's Somerset Park and conditions were as ripe as they could have been for an upset. But Rangers stuck to their task and got their goals at the right times. Ayr tried to harry Rangers out of their stride and although their tempo was the quicker, they couldn't carve out a clear-cut opportunity for an opening goal which could have changed the match. They knew that one lapse and the visitors would score, and that's exactly what happened after 14 minutes. Lorenzo Amoruso pumped a free-kick forward, and when it found Gabriel Amato, Steve Welsh was sticking to him like glue. But one quick turn and Amato was free and he drilled a 20-yard shot low into the net. Barry Ferguson was outstanding for Rangers and he was unlucky not to add to the lead with a 35-yard shot which Nelson did well to turn away.

Glynn Hurst had Ayr's best try at goal, with a shot from the edge of the box which Charbonnier tipped over brilliantly. But despite being the busier side, Ayr didn't really threaten the Rangers goal. Wallace and Amato both had chances to finish the tie, but Rangers had to wait until the 84th minute before they put it beyond doubt. Substitute Miller ran on to a van Bronckhorst corner on the edge of the box and cracked a first-time drive past Nelson. A potentially difficult tie was well negotiated.

Amato shoots to score the first goal of the match.

DUNDEE UTD 0   0 RANGERS

match highlights

Scottish Premier League
12 September 1998
Attendance: 12,788
Referee: J Rowbotham (Kirkcaldy)

Rangers' last Scottish Premier League match had been against Paul Sturrock's St Johnstone who had tried and failed to frustrate them at Ibrox. This time Paul Sturrock's Dundee United succeeded at Tannadice.

Most teams are desperate to impress a new manager and United looked no different in the early stages of this match. They pressed Rangers back in the opening exchanges and with the Rangers defence giving the ball away easily, Gary McSwegan broke clear but could only sweep his shot wide of Charbonnier's goal.

Rangers' best chance of the first half was when Ian Ferguson came close, with a curling shot which went inches over the top corner, after van Bonckhorst had found him at a free-kick. But it was again the former Ibrox man McSwegan who nearly made the breakthrough after 32 minutes with a fierce drive which brought a marvellous save from Charbonnier. This was a largely disappointing match, peppered with niggling bookings. United were out to contain Rangers, and the visitors had clearly left their creativity at home.

DUNDEE UTD

Dijkstra
Jenkins
Malpas
Olofsson
Zetterlund
McSwegan
McLaren
Duffy
Skoldmark
Mols
Patterson

substitutes
Combe
Easton
Miller

RANGERS

Charbonnier
Porrini
Amoruso
B Ferguson
Kanchelskis
Van Bronckhorst
Amato (Miller 71)
I Ferguson
Wallace
Moore
Vidmar

substitutes
Albertz
Graham
Miller

Rangers' Rod Wallace struggles to chip the ball over Dundee Utd keeper Dijkstra.

The Ibrox side didn't really deserve any more than they got from the match, although susbstitute Charlie Miller nearly got the winner with a close range effort which Dijkstra trapped with his legs. Dundee United may have got a point as a reward for their effort – but it didn't stop them going bottom that weekend.

BEITAR JERUSALEM 1   1 RANGERS

UEFA Cup 1st Round
1st Leg 15 September 1998
Attendance: 14,000
Referee: B Souse (France)

BEITAR JERUSALEM

Kornfein
Domb
Dery
Levy
Abukasis 16 (pen)
Telesnikov
Shelah
Shitrit
Hamar
Sandor
Rehuben (Raythman 35)

substitutes
Grif
Mizrahi
Ohama
Raythman
Yaacobi

RANGERS

Charbonnier
Porrini
Amoruso
B Ferguson
Kanchelskis
Van Bronckhorst
I Ferguson
Wallace (Graham 90)
Moore
Johansson (Albertz 78)
Vidmar (Stensaas 46)

substitutes
Albertz 84
Gattuso
Graham
Miller
Niemi
Petric
Stensaas

match highlights

There were rumours that Dick Advocaat didn't rate Jorg Albertz when he took over at Ibrox. If that was the case then evenings like these must have helped change his mind.

Rangers had a very uncomfortable night in Jerusalem, and were lucky to be only one goal down when the German came on as a substitute for Johansson with eight minutes to go. The Israelis had gone one up when the inventive Ofer Shitrit was adjudged to have been tripped by Charbonnier after 16 minutes and Abukasis had scored from the soft penalty award. They could have added to the lead had Shitrit been more incisive, first when he hesitated to let Porrini clear a far-post cross in the first half and then when he could only shoot at Charbonnier when clean through in the second.

The closest Rangers had come to scoring, until Albertz came on, was a first-half Porrini header which hit the bar. The introduction of the German was a last throw of the dice as Rangers searched for an equaliser – but it worked. He was on the field barely two minutes when Kanchelskis – who had had an ineffectual night – fed the ball into his path. Albertz didn't break stride and almost without looking up thundered a trademark shot from fully 25 yards which flew low into the right-hand corner of the net.

Rangers had looked as if only an inspirational moment of individual flair could save them – and Albertz had proved he was capable of providing it.

Jorg Albertz: the man who made it all happen by scoring a vital away goal in Europe.

RANGERS 0   0 CELTIC

match highlights

Scottish Premier League
20 September 1998
Attendance: 50,026
Referee: S Dougal (Glasgow)

No matter how hard Rangers pummelled their ancient rivals in this match, they just couldn't make the breakthrough. The Ibrox side dominated the 90 minutes, and although Celtic had a chance to sneak it at the last, this was two points dropped for Rangers.

The game started in the normal robust fashion, but it was Rangers who settled first. Jorg Albertz fired in a 30-yard free-kick after ten minutes which Gould couldn't hold, but the rebound didn't fall to a blue shirt. Fifteen minutes later and another shot hammered in by the German fizzed just wide. After 25 minutes came one of Rangers' best chances of the match – and a definitive moment in Gabriel Amato's first season.

RANGERS

Charbonnier
Porrini
Amoruso
B Ferguson
Kanchelskis (Graham 78)
Van Bronckhorst
Amato (Miller 69)
Albertz
Wallace
Moore
Hendry

substitutes
I Ferguson
Graham
Miller

Rod Wallace and the Rangers team played hard for 90 minutes but to no avail: they couldn't get through.

Van Bronckhorst split the Celtic defence with a superb pass, but with the fans on their feet anticipating a goal, Amato stumbled as he ran on to the ball and the chance was gone. In the second half Rangers carved out three more chances for Amato, but on each occasion the Argentinian couldn't convert them. It was a performance which badly damaged his reputation with the Rangers fans – and management. Van Bronckhorst tested Gould with two excellent long-range efforts, but it was a day when Rangers seemed destined to be frustrated. Amato was replaced by Charlie Miller after 68 minutes and one minute later Celtic almost took the lead. Amoruso was too casual and allowed Henrik Larsson through, but the Swede blazed the ball over the bar. Miller may have replaced Amato, but he had the luck of the Argentinian in front of goal. With ten minutes to go the midfielder rose unchallenged as van Bronckhorst swung in a corner. He powered a header down, but it bounced over the bar. Celtic had three chances to steal the match in the final frantic moments but Tosh McKinlay, Enrico Annoni and Alan Stubbs were all out of luck.

CELTIC

Gould
Boyd
Mahe
Rieper
Stubbs
Larsson
Burley
O'Donnell (McKinlay 83)
Donnelly
Jackson
Hannah (Annoni 84)

substitutes
Annoni
McKinlay
Kerr

ABERDEEN 1   1 RANGERS

Scottish Premier League
23 September 1998
Attendance: 17,862
Referee: W Young (Clarkston)

ABERDEEN

Leighton
Perry
Whyte
Inglis
Smith (Kiriakov 45)
Hignett
Jess 4
Dow (Gillies 88)
Buchan
Rowson
Winters (Newell 85)

substitutes
Gillies
Kiriakov
Newell

RANGERS

Charbonnier
Porrini
Amoruso
B Ferguson
Van Bronckhorst
Amato (Gattuso 87)
Albertz
Wallace 79
Moore
Vidmar (Johansson 61)
Miller (I Ferguson 61)

substitutes
I Ferguson
Gattuso
Johansson

match highlights

Rod Wallace hits Rangers' only goal. They had been behind for 75 minutes.

As ever, an Aberdeen side which had struggled against everyone else managed to find some form when they played Rangers.

On a tense night at Pittodrie the Dons took the lead after just three minutes and managed to hold onto it for the next 75. But Rangers battled for the entire 90 minutes and had more than enough chances to win the game. They hit the woodwork three times, and as happened so often in the first quarter of the League campaign, only bad luck and poor finishing stopped them taking all three points.

Colin Hendry missed this match with a foot injury and was replaced by Tony Vidmar, with Craig Moore and Lorenzo Amoruso linking up in the middle of defence. Charlie Miller started the game as a replacement for free-running midfielder Andrei Kanchelskis, who was suffering from a wrist injury.

Rangers found themselves 1-0 down after just three minutes. The Dons' new signing Robbie Winters got away from Moore, who tripped him up. Eoin Jess took an age over the free-kick, but when he struck the ball from 25 yards, it took a deflection off Gabriel Amato in the wall, spun beyond Lionel Charbonnier and landed in the back of the goal.

Stung by that, Rangers pinned the Dons back. Amoruso saw a net-bound header clawed away by Jim Leighton and then hit a post with a 30-yard shot. Wallace missed an easy chance after 25 minutes and then hit a post with an overhead kick as half-time approached.

After the break only a world-class save off the bendy legs of Leighton prevented Wallace from scoring after the 58th minute, as Rangers turned the screw. But the striker and his team mates had to wait for another 20 minutes before they were rewarded.

A Jorg Albertz pass found Wallace with his back to goal, but he turned on a sixpence, and slashed a shot high into the net for the equaliser.

DUNFERMLINE 0 2 RANGERS

match highlights

Scottish Premier League
26 September 1998
Attendance: 11,507
Referee: G Simpson (Westhill)

With Barry Ferguson the player of the moment, Dunfermline tried a unique tactic to stop him – they asked his brother Derek to mark him out of the match. It didn't work.

Barry the younger outplayed Derek the elder, as the current Ranger showed every sign of fulfilling the potential the ex-Ranger never did. They exchanged a couple of heavy tackles in the opening period but sensibly referee George Simpson left his cards in his pocket: better not to interfere in a domestic dispute. Barry ran the show again, but it was Jorg Albertz who created the opening goal after just 12 minutes. His through ball found Jonatan Johansson and he had plenty of time to drill the ball under Lee Butler and into the net.

It was young Barry though who secured the points with a beautiful goal four minutes after half-time. Sergio Porrini turned Marc Millar, and the Italian's pass was headed into Ferguson's path by Rod Wallace. Barry took just one touch and then fired a tremendous left-foot shot into the roof of the net from outside the box. Lorenzo Amoruso and Wallace both had chances to extend Rangers' lead, but the visitors took their foot off the gas and almost allowed Dunfermline to get back into it.

The Pars had a number of good efforts, the best when Derek Ferguson found Craig Ireland with a free-kick, but the centre-half's header was superbly saved – one-handed – by Charbonnier. It was to be Ferguson the younger's day.

'It was the first time I've ever played against Derek and it was a strange feeling'

— BARRY FERGUSON

DUNFERMLINE

Butler
Shields
McCulloch (Millar 46)
Ireland
French (Faulconbridge 79)
Huxford
Smith
Britton (Petrie 59)
Thomson
Squires
Ferguson

substitutes
Faulconbridge
Millar
Petrie

RANGERS

Charbonnier
Porrini
Amoruso
B Ferguson 49
Van Bronckhorst
Albertz
Wallace (Rozental 90)
Gattuso
Moore (Wilson 90)
Johansson 12 (I Ferguson 72)
Vidmar

substitutes
I Ferguson
Rozental
Wilson

Barry Ferguson rubbed salt into his Dunfermline-playing brother's wounds by scoring a goal.

RANGERS 4   2 BEITAR JERUSALEM

UEFA Cup 1st Round
2nd Leg 1 October 1998
Attendance: 45,610
Referee: S Khussainov (Russia)

RANGERS

Charbonnier
Porrini 25
Moore (Hendry 88)
Amoruso
Vidmar
Gattuso 1
B.Ferguson
Van Bronckhorst
Albertz
Wallace 65
Johansson 60 (Miller 80)

substitutes
Graham
Hendry
Miller
Niemi
Petric
Rozental
Stensaas

BEITAR JERUSALEM

Kornfein
Levy (Ohama 66)
Shelah
Dery
Telesnikov
Abukasis
Mizrahi
Salloi 34
Hamar
Sandor
Shitrit

substitutes
Gai
Ohama 80 (pen)
Raythman
Tretiak
Yaacobi

match highlights

Rangers almost looked like they could score at will in this match. The problem was they looked equally capable of giving away silly goals.

It should have been a much more straightforward night than it was when the home side went one up after just 20 seconds. It was a devastating move to start the match with: Amoruso fed the ball out to Albertz on the left, and he cleverly found Barry Ferguson inside him. Ferguson played the ball on to van Bronckhorst who hit a dangerous low cross into the box. Jonatan Johansson missed the ball by a whisker but when it ran through to Rino Gattuso making a late run, he crashed the ball into the roof of the net.

Johansson scored a goal on the 60-minute mark with a crafty chip over the Beitar keeper.

Rangers had the knack of swiftly changing pace and they cut the Beitar defence to ribbons at times, so it was ironic that the second goal came from a set piece after 25 minutes. Van Bronckhorst flighted in a corner from the left and Porrini darted into the box, past a defender, to head the ball into the net. That should have been the tie won, but Rangers allowed Beitar back into the match. Shitrit was given too much space on the left and as he ran into the box he slipped the ball to Salloi, who slid it into the net from a tight angle. Beitar gained a degree of composure from that strike and had the upper hand by half-time.

Rangers came out to kill off the tie quickly and on the hour mark got the security of a third goal. Vidmar was put clear by Barry Ferguson and made it to the bye-line. He cut the ball back and Johansson stuck out a leg and flicked the ball into the net. Rangers were back to free-flowing football, and within five minutes it brought them another goal. Albertz hit a wonderful long ball to Johansson who bore down on goal. He surged into the box but was pulled down by keeper Kornfein as he went round him. The referee however allowed play to go on, rather than giving a penalty, and Wallace rolled the ball into the empty net.

As thoughts turned to the next round, Rangers relaxed and allowed the visitors to threaten again: Sandor hit the bar with a fierce header and Ohama scored from the spot.

The result was never really in doubt – but it was a more awkward night for Rangers than it ought to have been.

RANGERS 1   0 DUNDEE

match highlights

Scottish Premier League
4 October 1998
Attendance: 48,348
Referee: K Clark (Paisley)

In the Scottish Cup the previous season, First Division Dundee had come and frustrated Walter Smith's Rangers in a 0-0 draw. Premier League Dundee would have done the same to Dick Advocaat's side had it not been for a blistering strike from Jorg Albertz 11 minutes from time. The German's spectacular shot from 35 yards seared past goalkeeper Robert Douglas who had looked unbeatable up until then.

Dundee had come to close down any space in the Rangers midfield, and managed to fashion a few opportunities of their own. But Douglas was their best player by far. He clawed out a net-bound header from Johansson after just one minute and when he blocked a Barry Ferguson 20-yarder after 20 minutes, the midfielder was reduced to punching the turf in frustration. Ferguson was again outstanding, but in the first half Dundee looked threatening as well. Twice Eddie Annand watched efforts flash just wide of Charbonnier's goal.

RANGERS

Charbonnier
Porrini
Amoruso
B Ferguson
Van Bronckhorst
Albertz 79
Wallace (I Ferguson 88)
Gattuso (Miller 45)
Johansson (Rozental 60)
Vidmar
Hendry

substitutes
I Ferguson
Miller
Rozental
Wilson

Barry Ferguson pumps a cross into the area. The game's only goal came from Jorg Albertz.

DUNDEE

Douglas
Smith
Adamczuk
Irvine
Raeside
Annand (Coyne 76)
Maddison (Anderson 84)
Falconer
McSkimming
Miller
Rae

substitutes
Anderson
Coyne
Grant
McInally

At half-time Advocaat decided to change things around. He brought on Charlie Miller for Gattuso and played him just behind the front two of Wallace and Amato, with Porrini moving into the right-hand side of midfield. Rangers had a better shape as a result, and camped themselves in the Dundee half for pretty much the remainder of the game. The visitor's goal was pummelled, with both the boot and the head of Albertz coming closest to the breakthrough. Still the goal eluded them and Seb Rozental was given a rare runout as Advocaat tried to vary things to get the winner.

Eventually Albertz scored, but Douglas salvaged some personal pride when he saved the German's penalty kick in the last minute after Miller had been brought down in the box.

RANGERS 3   0 HEARTS

Scottish Premier League
17 October 1998
Attendance: 49,749
Referee: S Dougal (Glasgow)

RANGERS

Charbonnier
Porrini
Amoruso ■
B Ferguson
Kanchelskis (Rozental 76)
Van Bronckhorst
Albertz
Wallace 61, 90 (Wilson 90)
Johansson 50 (Miller 65)
Vidmar
Hendry

substitutes
I Ferguson
Miller
Rozental
Wilson

HEARTS

Rousset
Naysmith
Weir ▯
Salvatori
Ritchie
Fulton ▯
Hamilton
Flogel (Guerin 45)
Pressley
Carricomdo (Makel 45)
McSwegan

substitutes
Guerin
Makel
McKenzie
Horn

match highlights

There were scores to settle at Ibrox when Hearts came to town. Having denied Rangers the Scottish Cup the previous May, the Edinburgh side had also inflicted a defeat on them on the opening day of the League season at Tynecastle.

Just to make sure there really was no love lost, Hearts manager Jim Jefferies had talked of his side winning the previous match comfortably, despite Rangers laying siege to their goal for most of the second half on the first day. Dick Advocaat, however, let his players do his talking for him on the pitch.

Revenge was well and truly got, and but for an inspired performance from Hearts keeper Gilles Rousset, the Tynecastle side would have been humiliated. In a goalless first half, the Frenchman denied Johansson, Kanchelskis and Amoruso when the efforts of all three looked goalbound. His most incredible stop came from Jorg Albertz. 'The Hammer' put his full force into a ten-yard blast, but somehow Rousset managed to athletically arch back to just get enough of a touch on the ball to palm it away.

Rangers were mauling the visitors, but they nearly let them in for an undeserved first strike when new signing Gary McSwegan got away from Amoruso and hit a drive against the post. But with pressure like this Hearts had to yield, and five minutes into the second half they did. Ferguson was fouled on the edge of the box, and when van Bronckhorst lifted the free-kick, Barry fired in a volley. Rousset parried it and when Wallace scuffed the rebound across the six yard box Johansson tucked the ball into the net for his fifth goal in seven starts.

Wallace added a second when a Johansson cross was deflected into his path by van Bronckhorst. The striker screwed his shot into the turf but it was enough to deceive Rousset who watched it trundle into the net off the post.

Amoruso was disappointingly sent off for a foul on Weir three minutes from time, but then ten-man Rangers added a superb third. Van Brockhorst lifted a ball over the Hearts defence and Wallace scampered onto it and drove the ball into the net. Hearts had been put in their place and Rangers were in theirs – two points clear of Kilmarnock at the top of the Premier League.

Jonathan Johansson slides in Rangers' first goal of the game.

BAYER LEVERKUSEN 1 2 RANGERS

match highlights

UEFA Cup 2nd Round
1st Leg 22 October 1998
Attendance: 22,000
Referee: K Bo Larsen (Denmark)

This was Rangers' first win in an away leg in Germany since 1961 – and one of their best ever results in Europe. They showed a maturity and a composure which not even a team like Bayer Leverkusen could shake them out of, and at times their passing was devastating. As expected, the Germans launched wave after wave of attack in the opening moments, but with a Rangers defence superbly marshalled by captain for the night Colin Hendry, they rarely created any openings.

Leverkusen coach Christophe Daum had identified Barry Ferguson as Rangers' most potent threat, and his fears were shown to be well founded when he created the opening goal in injury time just before the half-time break. Ferguson swivelled in the centre of midfield before dropping a perfectly-weighted pass into space which freed Johansson. The Finn passed the ball into the box and into the path of van Bronckhorst, who swept the ball into the net to give Rangers the lead at a critical stage. The Germans were stunned and the half-time break was not long enough for them to work out what was going wrong.

The second half started as the first had, with the Germans trying to apply pressure, but even when they did get threatening crosses into the box, there was no one on the end of them to make them count. The injured Ulf Kirsten was sorely missed by the home side. In the 63rd minute Rangers caught Leverkusen on the counter-attack. Van Bronckhorst picked up a loose ball in midfield and played it into space for Wallace. The Englishman scampered into the box, and although he could have had a shot himself, he squared the ball to Johansson who calmly slipped it into the net.

The 3,000 Rangers fans were ecstatic – and their team was in total command. Leverkusen had a goal chalked off for offside with 12 minutes to go, but they did manage a consolation from Reichenberger three minutes into injury time to give them a sliver of hope for the second leg.

BAYER LEVERKUSEN

Matysek
R Kovac
Happe (Reichenberger 76)
Reeb
Nowotny
Ze Roberto
Emerson (N Kovac 58)
Meijer
Rink
Beinlich
Ramelow (Heintze 58)

substitutes
Heintze
N Kovac
Lehnhoff
Mamic
Reichenberger 90
Vollborn
Zivkovic

RANGERS

Charbonnier
Porrini
B Ferguson
Kanchelskis
Van Bronckhorst 45
Albertz
Wallace (Durie 86)
Johansson 63 (I Ferguson 79)
Wilson
Vidmar
Hendry

substitutes
Amato
Durie
I Ferguson
Miller
Niemi
Petric
Stensaas

Van Bronckhorst played a hard game and was rewarded with a goal on the stroke of half time.

AIRDRIE 0   5 RANGERS

Scottish League Cup
Semi-final 25 October 1998
Attendance: 21,171
Referee: K Clark (Paisley)

AIRDRIE

Martin
Stewart
Jack (Evans 82)
Sandison
Smith
Black
Moore (Johnston 23)
Wilson
Cooper
McCann
McGrillen

substitutes
Evans
Farrell
Johnston

RANGERS

Charbonnier
Porrini
Wilson
Hendry
Vidmar
Kanchelskis
B Ferguson
Van Bronckhorst (Numan 73)
Albertz (I Ferguson 22)
Wallace 72, 77, 89
Johansson 6 (Durie 64)

substitutes
Durie
I Ferguson 34
Numan

match highlights

Such is their power that when Rangers flex their muscles, beating a team like Airdrie 5-0 is not unexpected. But while Rangers were that bit below par and perhaps didn't deserve to score five on the balance of play, poor defending from the Lanarkshire team made up for the Ibrox side's lack of finesse.

In a familiar story, Airdrie had to hold Rangers for as long as possible, just to have a realistic chance. They managed just six minutes before a blunder by keeper John Martin allowed Jonatan Johansson in to score.

With Airdrie taking no prisoners, the loss of the off-colour Jorg Albertz after 20 minutes was not as bad as it could have been – it meant that Ian Ferguson came on, and his presence balanced things up. Fergie in fact got the second goal which finished the match as a contest. Johansson swung over across from the right, and the long-serving midfielder met it with a flying header which bulleted past Martin.

In the second half Airdrie were full of energy but didn't have the craft to get a goal which could have brought them back into it. Instead they lost a third goal in the 72nd minute when Rod Wallace outpaced the Airdrie central defence to tuck away a long ball from Hendry.

Wallace repeated the trick six minutes later, turning in a beautiful ball from Durie as Rangers began to show their class. In the final minute Wallace was involved again, this time as provider, and when Durie ran onto his pass, he slipped the ball past Martin to celebrate his return to first-team action.

'I am happy with the result but we can play better than this. Airdrie worked so hard that they didn't give us time to think. We scored at the right moment and then they had to take more risks.'

— Dick Advocaat

Johansson kicks off the scoring, much to the dispair of the Airdrie number four.

MOTHERWELL 1   0 RANGERS

match highlights

Scottish Premier League
28 October 1998
Attendance: 11,777
Referee: E Martindale (Glasgow)

Having gone 17 games unbeaten, Rangers' run was to come to an end on a passionate night at Fir Park. Blame it on their hectic schedule or call it an off-day, but Rangers were outfought by a Motherwell side which had nothing to lose.

Inspired by a marvellous performance from ex-Ranger John Spencer – then on loan from Everton – Motherwell deserved their first win in seven games.

It was Spencer who got the winner with his debut goal after 55 minutes. Fellow new boy Ged Brannan chipped in a free-kick, and with some poor marking Spencer was allowed to turn and fire a drive into the net.

Rangers didn't create enough chances on a night when the entire team looked out of sorts and not in the mood for the sort of fight Motherwell were putting up. The Lanarkshire side scrapped for everything and knocked the visitors out of the smooth passing rhythm which had been a hallmark of previous games. The disjointed performance was summed up by a moment five minutes before Motherwell scored. Rod Wallace burst through the home defence, but when he centred both Kanchelskis and Johansson left the ball for each other, and neither one took it.

Both Numan and Ian Ferguson should have done better than to shoot over the bar as Rangers pressed madly in the last ten minutes, but in the end Motherwell got the victory they deserved.

MOTHERWELL

Kaven
McMillan
McGowan
Brannan
Valakari
Coyle
Christie
Doesburg
Teale
Adams (McCulloch 66)
Spencer 55 (Nevin 66)

substitutes
May
McCulloch
Nevin
Woods

RANGERS

Charbonnier
Porrini
Amoruso
B Ferguson
Kanchelskis
Van Bronckhorst
Albertz (Durie 45)
Wallace
Johansson (I Ferguson 60)
Vidmar (Numan 45)
Hendry

substitutes
Durie
I Ferguson
Numan
Brown

Colin Hendry – along with the rest of the team – had a disappointing game.

RANGERS 2   1 DUNDEE UNITED

Scottish Premier League
31 October 1998
Attendance: 49,503
Referee: J McCluskey (Stewarton)

RANGERS

Charbonnier
Porrini
Amoruso 84
Ferguson
Kanchelskis
Van Bronckhorst
Amato (Graham 84)
Albertz
Wallace 63
Vidmar (Numan 45)
Hendry

substitutes
Graham
Niemi
Numan
Wilson

DUNDEE UNITED

Dijkstra
Malpas
Jonsson
Patterson
Olofsson (Thompson 88)
Zetterlund
Easton
Mathie (Paterson 87)
Dodds 25
Skoldmark (Miller 87)
Pascual

substitutes
Combe
Miller
Paterson
Thompson

match highlights

Rangers captain Lorenzo Amoruso did not have the best possible start to the season: a few moments of uncertainty and a couple of mistakes had brought derision from the majority of the press as well as the stands.

But this match turned out to be symbolic of his entire season. He made a mistake in the first half which saw the opposition take the lead – but he capped an inspirational performance in the second by scoring the winning goal.

Amoruso failed to clear his own area after 25 minutes and allowed Billy Dodds to chip Lionel Charbonnier and give the Tannadice side a shock lead. United could have increased it five minutes later, but Olofsson made a hash of a chance close in.

It was a different Rangers side in attitude and personnel which appeared for the second half, with Numan replacing Vidmar. Immediately Rangers started pressing, but there was good fortune when they finally made the breakthrough. Numan found Hendry with a cross, but when the defender tried to shoot he only succeeded in placing the ball at the feet of Rod Wallace. Showing a striker's instinct he flashed a low drive into the net from five yards for his 12th goal of the season.

Rangers immediately looked for the winner and Hendry came close with a header. But it was his defensive partner who was to get the vital goal. With just six minutes remaining, van Bronckhorst swung in a corner and Amoruso made amends for his earlier lapse by heading the ball low into the net for the winner. The victory kept Rangers one point ahead of Kilmarnock at the top of the Premier League after a run of four games in ten days.

In a spirited game, the Gers pulled through to win with a goal from Amoruso in the 84th minute.

RANGERS 1   1 BAYER LEVERKUSEN

match highlights

UEFA Cup 2nd Round
2nd Leg 5 November 1998
Attendance: 50,012
Referee: L Batista (Portugal)

There was no white flag raised by Bayer Leverkusen after their first leg defeat. Instead that result was like a red rag to a bull. They charged at Rangers from the very start of the return leg and had the upper hand for most of the match.

Twice Erik Meijer bore down on goal in the opening minutes only to be denied, first by the brilliance of Charbonnier, and then by his own lack of composure. At the other end Rangers had a penalty claim turned down when Nowotny seemed to handle a Kanchelskis cross, but it was the visitors who were the more threatening side. A Heintze cross was cut out by Hendry with Meijer lurking, before Heintze went for goal himself with a 25-yard shot which Charbonnier could only punch away.

Rangers were relieved to be on level terms at the break, but within 11 minutes of the second half they were in the lead thanks to a mistake from the Germans. Amoruso thumped the ball forward towards Johansson. Heintze tried to clear it but only succeeded in playing it into the Rangers striker's path. Johansson sprinted forward, cut inside from the left and cracked a 20-yard shot beyond Matysek and into the net.

Charbonnier had to be replaced by Niemi after 67 minutes after he collided with a post, falling awkwardly and damaging ligaments in his knee. It was to be the Frenchman's last match of the season because of the injury.

Ibrox nerves were calmed by the goal, but jangled again when the Germans equalised with just 12 minutes to go. Ramelow crossed from the left, and when substitute Reichenberger fed the ball on to Kirsten, he clipped it into the net with ease. Rangers then had to endure an anxious closing period but they held onto to go on to the last 16 of the UEFA Cup.

Arthur Numan goes on the offensive, chased by an opponent. Solid play – and a little luck – had seen Rangers through.

RANGERS

Charbonnier (Niemi)
Porrini
Hendry
Amoruso
Numan
Kanchelskis (I Ferguson 67)
B Ferguson (Wilson 90)
Van Bronckhorst
Albertz
Wallace
Johansson 56

substitutes
Amato
I Ferguson
Miller
Niemi
Petric
Vidmar
Wilson

BAYER LEVERKUSEN

Matysek
R Kovac (Emerson 39)
Happe
Reeb
Nowotny
Ze Roberto
Kirsten 79
Meijer (N Kovac 77)
Heintze (Reichenberger 66)
Beinlich
Ramelow

substitutes
Emerson
N Kovac
Mamic
Reichenberger
Rink
Vollborn
Zivkovic

ST JOHNSTONE 0   7 RANGERS

Scottish Premier League
8 November 1998
Attendance: 9,636
Referee: K Clark (Paisley)

ST JOHNSTONE

Main
McQuillan
Dasovic
Kernaghan
O'Neil
O'Boyle (Grant 79)
Kane ▌
McMahon (McCluskey 69)
Bollan ▌
Dods
Lowndes (Griffin 45)

substitutes
Grant ▌
Griffin
McCluskey

RANGERS

Niemi
Numan (Miller 72)
Kanchelskis 64
Van Bronckhorst
Albertz 31, 82 (pens)
Amoruso
Ferguson
Wallace 10
Johansson 29 (Guivarc'h 68)
Vidmar
Hendry (Wilson 45)

substitutes
Amato
Guivarc'h 70, 79
Miller
Wilson

match highlights

If first impressions really meant anything then Stephane Guivarc'h would still be at Ibrox. The Frenchman made his debut in Perth after his £3.5 million move from Newcastle and scored two excellent goals as Rangers savaged St Johnstone 7–0.

The match was supposed to be a rehearsal of the League Cup Final but there was no holding back from the Ibrox side. Dick Advocaat was forced to make changes to the normal line-up: Charbonnier was to miss the rest of the season through injury, while Barry Ferguson and Sergio Porrini were also sidelined. Antti Niemi, Ian Ferguson and Tony Vidmar replaced them. Rangers, however, settled quickly and were one up after ten minutes.

A thunderbolt from Jorg Albertz was tipped over by Alan Main. Van Bronckhorst swung over the corner, Vidmar chested it on and Wallace flicked it over the line with his head. Main clawed the ball out but it had already crossed the line.

St Johnstone's pace up front was a threat but they were disorganised in defence. Rangers again took advantage when van Bronckhorst's 29th minute shot was parried by Main and Johansson rammed in the rebound for his ninth goal in 11 games.

Two minutes later the match was over as a contest with Rangers three up and St Johnstone reduced to ten men. Van Bronckhorst was brought down in the box by Paul Kane, and although it was definitely a penalty, the Saints man was very unlucky to be red-carded. Albertz scored from the spot. Wallace had a goal disallowed for offside in the 42nd minute, and it took until the

Guivarc'h and his fellow Rangers in red celebrate another mark on the scoresheet.

64th minute for number four to arrive. Kanchelskis picked up the ball on the right and cut inside along the 18 yard line, before unleashing a low left foot shot into the net.

Guivarc'h replaced Johansson in the 66th minute and it took him just four minutes to add his name to the scoresheet. Van Bronckhorst played a pass in to him from the edge of the box, Guivarc'h spun and shot in one exquisite movement. The ball took a slight deflection off a defender before spinning over Main. Things were to get even worse for the Saints. Kanchelskis played a cross into the box from the right, and it was Guivarc'h again who chested the ball down and sent a low left foot shot past Main for his second, and Rangers' sixth, goal. Two minutes later it was 7-0. Van Bronckhorst was brought down by John O'Neil and Albertz slammed the kick home from the spot.

RANGERS 2 1 ABERDEEN

match highlights

Scottish Premier League
14 November 1998
Attendance: 49,479
Referee: H Dallas (Motherwell)

Johansson played only 45 minutes but it was enough time to make a significant impact on the game.

RANGERS

Niemi
Porrini
Numan
▌ Hendry
B Ferguson
Kanchelskis 82
▌ Van Bronckhorst 8
Albertz (I Ferguson 70)
Wallace
Johansson (Guivarc'h 45)
Wilson

substitutes
I Ferguson
Guivarc'h
Nicholson

ABERDEEN

Leighton
Perry
Whyte
Smith
▌ Hignett
Jess 56
▌ Newell
Kiriakov (Hart 88)
Anderson
Rowson
Winters

substitutes
Dow
Hart
Inglis
Stillie

Rangers failed to capitalise on long periods of pressure and had to thank a Jim Leighton blunder for the three points which saw them go ten points clear at the top of the Premier League.

With just eight minutes left and the match tied at 1-1, Andrei Kanchelskis went on a run down the right before cutting inside – across the face of the penalty area – and firing in a left foot drive. Leighton, who was all that stood between Aberdeen and a rout, tried to stop the ball with his legs, but it went under him and into the net for the winner.

Rangers should have had the game won long before then. They got off to a great start when van Bronckhorst gave them the lead after just eight minutes. The midfielder picked the ball up on the left and hit a diagonal drive from the edge of the box and into the corner of the net. Only fine saves from Johansson and Porrini stopped Rangers surging further ahead. But Rangers' rearguard, with Scott Wilson in for the suspended Amoruso, looked vulnerable at times, and Niemi did well to stand up and deny Jess a breakaway goal.

A Rod Wallace drive felled Leighton when it caught him in the face but on the stroke of half-time Craig Hignett nearly pinched an equaliser but was denied by Niemi. It was a warning which Rangers didn't heed.

Eleven minutes after the break Aberdeen drew level when Mike Newell laid the ball off to Jess who drove it past Niemi and into the net. Jess came close to putting the Dons into the lead moments later, but this time his drive was just wide. Guivarc'h had come on for Johansson at half-time and was unfortunate to see a shot kicked off the line by Newell. Rangers pressed for the winner in a frantic final spell and after van Bronckhorst saw a late shot held by Leighton, Anderson almost deflected a Kanchelskis cross past his own keeper. Then, in the 82nd minute, Kanchelskis thundered in a shot, Leighton blundered and Rangers took all three points.

CELTIC 5   1 RANGERS

Scottish Premier League
21 November 1998
Attendance: 59,703
Referee: W Young (Clarkston)

CELTIC

Warner
Boyd
Mahe
Stubbs ▨
Larsson 51, 57
O'Donnell
Donnelly (Hannah 79)
Lambert
Moravcik 11, 49 (Burchill 82)
Riseth
Mjallby

substitutes
Annoni
Brattbakk
Burchill 89
Hannah

RANGERS

Niemi
Porrini
Numan ▨
B Ferguson (I Ferguson 74)
Kanchelskis (Vidmar 61)
Van Bronckhorst 53
Albertz (Durie 61)
Guivarc'h
Wallace
Wilson ▮
Hendry ▨

substitutes
Durie
Vidmar
I Ferguson
Nicholson

match highlights

Celtic had to win this game to make the championship a race, or risk falling 13 points behind Rangers. For the Ibrox side this was an afternoon best forgotten.

Nothing went right and they were one down within 11 minutes. Simon Donnelly made a break down the left and crossed. Henrik Larsson dummied to let the ball go through to Lubomir Moravcik who swept the ball into the net from the edge of the area.

Rangers could have come back from that, but the sky started to fall in when Scott Wilson was sent off in a moment of rashness. Wilson, deputising for suspended captain Lorenzo Amoruso, made a late challenge on goalscorer Moravcik and when Referee Young pulled out the red card Rangers were left to play 68 minutes with just ten men. Celtic were showing the kind of form that had eluded them so far this season and after the interval went for the kill. In a frenetic eight minute period four goals were scored – three by Celtic, one by Rangers.

Van Bronckhorst salvages something from a dismal match, but not nearly enough.

Moravcik got his second, heading in a Tom Boyd cross after 49 minutes. Then Donnelly put Larsson through after 51 minutes and his clinical finish put Celtic three up. Two minutes later, Rangers got a free-kick. Van Bronckhorst curled it beyond the wall and goalkeeper Warner and into the net off the post. It was a tremendous strike – but one that would be sadly forgotten because of the circumstances.

Instead of sparking a comeback, that goal was an early consolation. Things got worse when Larsson headed in an O'Donnell cross to make it 4–1 after 57 minutes. Guivarc'h should have pulled one back when he was given a free header four minutes later, but he nodded wide. With the Rangers rearguard tiring, Celtic got their embarrassing fifth. Burchill – who had replaced Moravcik – ran onto a ball from Larsson and tucked it into the net.

RANGERS 1   1 PARMA

match highlights

UEFA Cup 3rd Round
1st Leg 24 November 1998
Attendance: 49,514
Referee: A Sars (France)

Rangers have major ambitions in Europe, and playing Parma must be one of the best yardsticks to measure yourself against.

At first outplayed by the Italians, when the Ibrox side got in to the pace of the game they thoroughly deserved their draw and could have even won had Gordon Durie been a bit more lucky in the closing minutes. Parma were the dominant side in the first 45 minutes and Rangers were lucky to go in at the break on level terms. But somehow when the Italians took the lead six minutes into the second half, it was the spur which the home side needed to stop standing back and to start competing.

Parma's slick passing brought a reward when the Rangers defence couldn't handle the movement of Abel Balbo who forced his way into the box to score from close range. There was no point in Rangers playing a waiting game now, and Dick Advocaat moved to three at the back, bringing on an extra attacker, Durie, for Sergio Porrini. It meant Rangers were exposed at times but the extra pressure they exerted up front bore fruit.

In the 69th minute Barry Ferguson pumped in a cross from the right and when Colin Hendry headed it down, Rod Wallace was there to clip the ball into the net. Rangers may not have had the poise of Parma, but the Italian team didn't have the spirit of the Scots.

They continued to attack after the equaliser, with Parma always ready to counter and the match reached a frantic pace in the last few minutes. In injury time Amato whipped in a cross, Durie rose to meet it but could only head wide. As Rangers fans thought they had been robbed of victory, Niemi pulled off a marvellous save from Stefano Fiore to avoid defeat. Honours even, but Rangers had grown as the match had worn on.

RANGERS

Niemi
Porrini (Durie 58)
Amoruso
Hendry
Numan
B Ferguson
Kanchelskis
Albertz
I Ferguson
Wallace 69
Johansson (Amato 46)

substitutes
Amato
Brown
Durie
Miller
Stensaas
Vidmar
Wilson

PARMA

Buffon
Bennarivo
Sartor
Baggio
Crespo (Orlandini 90)
Veron (Fiore 70)
Stanic
Boghossain
Cannavaro
Balbo 51
Thuram

substitutes
Fiore
Giunti
Guardalden
Orlandini
Pedros
Sensini
Vanol

Andrei Kanchelskis shows exactly why he is worth big money in the European transfer market.

Scottish Football League Cup Final
29 November 1998
Attendance: 45,533
Referee: H Dallas (Motherwell)

RANGERS

Niemi
Porrini
Amoruso
Hendry
Numan
B Ferguson
Kanchelskis
Van Bronckhorst
Guivarc'h 6 (Durie 89)
Wallace
Albertz 37 (I Ferguson 65)

substitutes
Durie
I Ferguson
Vidmar

Scottish Football League Cup Final

When you have gorged on silverware the way that Rangers fans have over the last decade you can become addicted. After a trophyless season last term they were showing signs of withdrawal symptoms, but Dick Advocaat provided them with the quickest fix he could – the Scottish League Cup.

The St Johnstone side they had so recently mauled 7-0 were the opponents, and they were naturally determined to prevent a repeat of a scoreline anything like that. But for the second match in succession at Celtic Park, Rangers benefited from a goalkeeping error after just six minutes to take the lead. Sergio Porrini flighted a ball in from the left and Saints keeper Alan Main froze as Andrei Kanchelskis nipped in front of Gary Bollan to pick it up. Kanchelskis was allowed to make it to the byeline from where he cut the ball back into the path of Guivarc'h who slammed it past Main for the third time in his short career at Ibrox.

It would have been easy for St Johnstone to have crumbled. The memories of the drubbing at McDiarmid Park were very fresh. But to their credit the Perth side got back on level terms within two minutes. Midfielder Paul Kane lofted a free-kick into the Rangers box, and when Alan Kernaghan nodded the ball down on the edge of the box, Nick Dasovic was there on the edge of the box to unleash a vicious shot which went into the roof of the net.

Albertz cuts his way through the St Johnstone defence on his way to scoring another quality goal.

1   ST JOHNSTONE

match highlights

Scottish Football League Cup Final
29 November 1998
Attendance: 45,533
Referee: H Dallas (Motherwell)

The goal gave Saints the confidence they needed and Kane and Dasovic began to have the upper hand in midfield. They combined to put Phil Scott through, but he was un-nerved by the advancing Niemi and shot weakly into the goalkeeper's arms. It was Rangers who looked unsettled now, but nothing settles a team like a goal and they got what turned out to be the decisive one after 37 minutes. It showed a rare delicate side to Jorg Albertz's nature – as well as his brutal power. The German stepped over a pass from Barry Ferguson to allow it to roll through to Guivarc'h. The Frenchman stroked it back in front of Albertz and he thundered in a first-time shot which flew past Main into the net.

The Rangers ship had been steadied and they were to allow St Johnstone only one more opportunity in the entire match. Ten minutes into the second half, George O'Boyle missed a dramatic overhead kick, and Kane could only smack the ball wide when it fell to him. Rangers were in control from then on, but never threatened to run riot as they had done in previous meetings.

Kanchelskis could have made it 3-1 with a volley with nine minutes to go, but Main denied him with a save which showed the keeper's true abilities. But Rangers had won the Cup without ever hitting the heights of their previous encounters with St Johnstone, or playing particularly well at all. But it was enough for them to win the League Cup for the 21st time, and the cupboard at Ibrox was no longer bare.

Dick Advocaat stood with his hands in his pockets, having a chat with Bert van Lingen as the players celebrated. Perhaps he was unmoved. Perhaps he was relieved that a trophy had been won so quickly. Or perhaps he was planning on winning bigger prizes.

ST JOHNSTONE

Main
McQuillan
Dasovic 8
Kernaghan
Scott
O'Neil
O'Boyle (Lowndes 74)
Kane
Bollan
Dods
Simao (Grant 84)

substitutes
Grant
Lowndes
Preston

The team celebrate what they hoped would be the first of many trophies. It was.

THE SCOTTISH FOOTBALL LEAGUE CUP WINNERS 1998

RANGERS 1 1 DUNFERMLINE

Scottish Premier League
5 December 1998
Attendance: 47,465
Referee: W Young (Clarkston)

RANGERS

Niemi
Porrini
Amoruso
Numan
Hendry
B Ferguson
Kanchelskis
Van Bronckhorst 16
Albertz
Guivarc'h (Durie 71)
Wallace

substitutes
Durie
I Ferguson
Miller

DUNFERMLINE

Butler
Shields
McCulloch
Tod
French
Huxford
Smith
Johnson
Edinho (Millar 63)
Graham (Petrie 72)
Ferguson (Fraser 90)

substitutes
Fraser
Millar
Petrie 76

match highlights

Rangers seemed all at sea to their title challengers when they threw away two points against a struggling Dunfermline side. Despite dominating the match, they could take only one of the many chances they created. The Fifers were content to put all their men behind the ball and hope they would take their chance if it came. It did.

After an uncertain start when the Rangers defence again looked vulnerable, the home side settled and took the lead. Kanchelskis thundered in a drive but when it was blocked by former Ranger Greg Shields, van Bronckhorst was on hand to drive the rebound into the net. That should have been the first of many goals, but Rangers squandered their chances. Guivarc'h was twice denied by Butler, but after the break the Frenchman was desperately unlucky to see an instinctive left foot volley go inches wide.

Dunfermline brought on Marc Millar and Stewart Petrie for Edinho and David Graham as they searched for the equaliser, while Rangers sent on Gordon Durie for Guivarc'h to look for the goal to finish the match.

With 14 minutes left it was the Fifers' changes which paid off. Derek Ferguson lumped a hopeful free-kick into the penalty box. It found his brother Barry who failed to control it and the ball bounced off his knee and into the path of Petrie who smashed it past Niemi. The draw saw Rangers' lead at the top of the League reduced to just goal difference over Kilmarnock.

Frenchman Stephane Guivarc'h was always in the thick of the action but failed to convert any chances.

PARMA 3 | 1 RANGERS

match highlights

UEFA Cup 3rd Round
2nd Leg 8 December 1998
Attendance: 17,000
Referee: T Hauge (Norway)

Rangers may have a foreign coach and have a majority of foreign players, but they managed to produce another old-fashioned tale of glorious failure – like so many Scottish sides before them. They had the chance to pull off an incredible win and then shot themselves in the foot. Early on though, it was the Italian side which was making mistakes, and Rangers capitalised after 28 minutes. Sensini was sloppy with a pass out of defence and played the ball straight to Albertz. The German powered his way forward before cracking a shot low into the back of the net.

Rangers contained Parma from that point but were dealt a dreadful blow when Porrini was sent off for his second bookable offence in injury time at the break. Porrini tripped Juan Veron only two minutes after he had been harshly booked for an earlier challenge on the Argentinian. Nonetheless he was off, and somehow holding the lead didn't mean so much – nor did it last. Two minutes into the second half, slack defending in the hole on the right, which Porrini had left, saw Parma sweep through the gap and Balbo equalised with a tap-in.

Technically, Rangers were still on level terms in the tie, but in truth they were being swept aside. Their poise and organisation had gone. Stefano Fiore – a substitute for Alain Boghossian – effectively settled the tie in the 63rd minute with a fierce shot which gave Niemi no chance. An equaliser would, of course, have put Rangers through on away goals, but the chances of that were snuffed out by a moment of madness from Lorenzo Amoruso. The Rangers captain palmed away a pass by Juan Veron inside his own box. Even though Chiesa was chasing the ball, there seemed little real danger to justify his action. Chiesa scored from the spot and in the end Rangers were happy to keep the score down to three.

They had put on a marvellous display in the first half, but it all unravelled after Porrini was sent off.

PARMA

Buffon
Thuram
Sensini
Cannavaro
Fuser (Mussi 84)
Baggio
Boghossian (Fiore 56)
Bennarivo
Veron
Balbo 47
Chiesa 66 (pen) (Crespo 74)

substitutes
Crespo
Fiore 63
Mussi

RANGERS

Niemi
Porrini
Hendry
Amoruso
Numan
Albertz 29
B Ferguson (Miller 81)
I Ferguson
Van Bronckhorst
Wallace (Amato 73)
Durie (Vidmar 54)

substitutes
Amato
Miller
Vidmar

Jorg Albertz: back on form to score the goal that put Rangers into the lead.

RANGERS 1   0 KILMARNOCK

Scottish Premier League
12 December 1998
Attendance: 49,781
Referee: J Rowbotham (Kirkcaldy)

RANGERS

Niemi
Porrini
Amoruso
Numan (Vidmar 28)
Hendry
B Ferguson (I Ferguson 71)
Kanchelskis
Van Bronckhorst
Albertz
Guivarc'h (Durie 61)
Wallace 10

substitutes
Durie
I Ferguson
Vidmar

KILMARNOCK

Marshall
MacPherson
Montgomerie
McGowne
Reilly
Holt
Wright (McCoist 75)
Durrant
Mitchell (Roberts 75)
Vareille (Mahood 18)
Baker

substitutes
McCoist
Mahood
Roberts

match highlights

Rangers got their title challenge back on track with a result which was much more pleasing than the performance.

With just goal difference separating the two sides at the top of the SPL, a tenth-minute goal from Rod Wallace was enough to secure the victory. Barry Ferguson was once again the provider. He took the ball down the right before curling in a neatly-judged cross. Wallace chopped his stride as he ran on to the ball before unleashing a left-foot volley which sent it into the net. The home side could have been one down rather than one up at that stage. Kevin McGowne lofted a harmless-looking ball forward in the opening moments but when van Bronckhorst and Amoruso got into a fankle, Jerome Vareille was allowed through but could only shoot straight at Niemi.

Rangers responded immediately, but when Guivarc'h's volley found the net moments later it was ruled out for offside. Vareille had to go off with a shoulder injury after 18 minutes, and with him went Killie's goal chances. Rangers' Arthur Numan also had to be replaced after 28 minutes and it turned out to be his last match of the season. Rangers had more of the play in midfield, but this was a game which never lived up to its top-of-the-table-clash billing. Goal opportunites were few and far between.

Kanchelskis did carve out a chance for Albertz in the 57th minute but the German's volley was well saved by Marshall. This was Rangers' 31st match of fixture-crammed season and fatigue was beginning to tell in their performance. The important thing was the result.

Guivarc'h, Barry Ferguson, Numan and Wallace all celebrate the goal that won the game.

HEARTS 2 3 RANGERS

match highlights

Scottish Premier League
19 December 1998
Attendance: 17,134
Referee: S Dougal (Glasgow)

'It was an excellent result because this is a difficult fixture. We dominated for 75 minutes but lost the first goal because our defenders were watching each other and not picking up Hearts players.'

— DICK ADVOCAAT

There had been the fear amongst Rangers supporters that adopting the continental apporach under Dick Advocaat would mean that the team's traditional fighting qualities would take a back seat. That was disproved at Tynecastle as Rangers won another difficult away fixture to give themselves a cushion at the top as the winter break beckoned. But they were made to fight for it.

A reshuffled Rangers line-up with Tony Vidmar and Stale Stensaas in for the injured Arthur Numan and Colin Hendry were one down after just two minutes. Thomas Flogel got past both Vidmar and Amoruso and his near-post cross was headed home by Hearts captain Gary Locke for his first goal in 30 months.

Tynecastle was a cauldron and the home side had the upper hand in the early stages but they didn't knock Rangers off their stride. Niemi produced two excellent saves to deny Jim Hamilton before Rousset had to be at his best to turn over a shot from Albertz.

Rangers survived the Hearts storm and equalised in the 16th minute with a classic counter-attack. Stensaas found himself unmarked on the left and when he found Guivarc'h, the Frenchman had plenty of time to pick his spot past Rousset.

The goal increased the frantic pace of the game and, while there was little time for passing football, there was plenty of excitement at both ends. Ian Ferguson came on for Stensaas at half time and immediately Rangers had more bite in midfield. Albertz came close with a shot and a Guivarc'h drive was cleared off the line.

Then Rangers took the lead. After 60 minutes Weir couldn't cut out a through ball from Albertz and Rod Wallace ran on to it to fire home from 16 yards. Five minutes later Rangers were 3-1 up, when Guivarc'h again found time in the box and impudently drove the ball low and in, past Rousset at his near post. Hearts stormed back, and Flogel was again the provider when he found Hamilton inside the box, and the striker volleyed home from ten yards for a spectacular goal. Neil McCann came on for the last 11 minutes to makes his debut at the club he had just left.

The Edinburgh team battled for the equaliser, and although Flogel and Adam went close, Rangers held on for an excellent win.

Stephane Guivarc'h celebrates with outstretched arms as he scored what turned out to be the winning goal.

HEARTS

Rousset
McPherson
Weir
Ritchie
Fulton
Adam (Juanjo 75)
Hamilton 68
Locke 2 (Quitongo 82)
Flogel
McKinnon
Murray (Makel 70)

substitutes
Juanjo
Makel
Quitongo

RANGERS

Niemi
Porrini
Amoruso
Kanchelskis
Van Bronckhorst
Albertz
Guivarc'h 16, 63
Wallace 58
Stensaas (I Ferguson 45)
Vidmar
B Ferguson (McCann 79)

substitutes
I Ferguson
McCann

RANGERS 1   0 ST JOHNSTONE

Scottish Premier League
26 December 1998
Attendance: 49,479
Referee: A Freeland (Aberdeen)

RANGERS

Klos
Porrini 71 ▪
Amoruso
Hendry ▪
B Ferguson
Kanchelskis (McCann 48)
Van Bronckhorst
Albertz
Guivarc'h (Wilson 70)
Wallace (Miller 90)
Vidmar ▪

substitutes
McCann
Miller
Wilson

St JOHNSTONE

Main
McQuillan
Dasovic
Kernaghan ▪
O'Neil
Kane
McMahon (Lowndes 86)
Connolly (Grant 60)
Bollan
McAnespie ▪ (Simao 68)
Dods

substitutes
Grant
Lowndes
Simao

match highlights

Rangers got out of jail on Boxing Day as St Johnstone missed their best chance for their first win at Ibrox since 1971.

Having had the best of the game in the first 45 minutes, the Ibrox side were disppointed to go in on even terms at the break. If they had been unlucky not to score in the first half, they were very fortunate to deny Sandy Clark's side in the second.

With the game still goalless just thee minutes after half-time, Paddy Connolly ran onto a through ball, rounded Stefan Klos and fired the ball at goal. Colin Hendry blocked the first shot with his feet, but when the rebound found the Saints striker again, the Scotland captain could only stop his second effort with his hand. It was a clear penalty and Hendry was sent off. But when John O'Neil crashed the spot kick off the bar Rangers' luck turned. Reduced to ten men, Rangers lost their shape a little and let the Saints have a period of pressure which almost told. Kernaghan had a shot kicked off the line by Kanchelskis before Dasovic hit the bar. It looked to be a further blow to the home side when Kanchelskis had to limp off, but as his replacement McCann had a hand in the only goal of the game, it turned out to be a blessing in disguise.

Sergio Porrini moved forward onto a pass from Ferguson and freed McCann on the wing. He held onto it for only a couple of touches before feeding it back into the Italian's path and he drilled the ball high into the net from 15 yards. The Saints pressed towards the end, but Stefan Klos was in no mood to concede a goal on his debut.

Advocaat was relieved with the victory. He said: 'I'm pleased to win under the circumstances. We were the better side in the first half but it changed after Hendry was sent off. But I thought it was an excellent save from him!'

Kanchelskis was on the receiving end of some tough play.

DUNDEE UNITED 1 2 RANGERS

match highlights

Scottish Premier League
30 December 1998
Attendance: 11,707
Referee: M McCurry (Glasgow)

A last-minute goal from Rod Wallace meant that Rangers maintained their ten-point lead over Celtic going into the New Year Old Firm clash, as Rangers survived a dour and physical encounter at Tannadice.

It was not a pretty game as United tried to block Rangers at every turn, and the Ibrox side's creative players were subdued by the sheer workrate of the opposition.

Neil McCann started his first game for the Light Blues, but it was defender Scott Wilson – in for the suspended Hendry – who made the most significant impact.

In a game of few opportunities, Rangers got a corner on the right just after the half-hour mark. The United defence couldn't clear their lines properly, and when Wallace pumped the ball back into the box, Wilson rose high and powered a header down which took a deflection off Jason de Vos on its way into the net.

The goal spurred United into action and they got an equaliser just before half-time – again because of a corner which wasn't cleared properly. Miller delivered the ball in from the left and it was knocked out only as far as de Vos on the edge of the box. His pass found Billy Dodds in plenty of space and he picked his spot past Klos.

The second half was as ugly as the first, with every cross and every potential chance-making pass seeming to be just an inch away from a striker. With it looking as though United's hard work would be rewarded with a point, Rangers struck in the dying minutes.

Johansson – on as a replacement for McCann – made a powerful run down the left, beating three defenders on his way. He laid the ball off to Amato, and when he crossed this time he found Wallace unmarked and in plenty of space, and the striker thumped the ball into the net for a vital winner.

DUNDEE UNITED

Combe
Malpas
Pedersen
Easton
Mathie
Dodds 43
Miller
Duffy
De Vos
Mols
Pascual

substitutes

RANGERS

Klos
Porrini
Amoruso
B Ferguson
Van Bronckhorst
Albertz (Miller 71)
Guivarc'h (Amato 35)
Wallace 90
McCann (Johansson 75)
Wilson 32
Vidmar

substitutes
Amato
Johansson
Miller

Johansson and Wallace congratulate each other on another goal.

RANGERS 2   2 CELTIC

Scottish Premier League
3 January 1999
Attendance: 50,059
Referee: J McCluskey (Stewarton)

RANGERS

Klos
Porrini
Amoruso
Hendry
B Ferguson
Kanchelskis (Albertz 61)
Van Bronckhorst
Amato 45
Wallace 58
McCann (Johansson 72)
Vidmar

substitutes
Albertz
Johansson
Miller

CELTIC

Gould
Boyd
Mahe
McNamara
Stubbs 39
Larsson 66
O'Donnell
Lambert
Moravcik
Riseth
Mjallby

substitutes

match highlights

It wasn't a classic for the purist, but in terms of excitement the third Old Firm match of the season couldn't be beaten. It was the last game before the winter shutdown and there was even more at stake than usual. Rangers, ten points clear, wanted to gain revenge for the 5-1 hammering they had taken at Celtic Park and to give Dick Advocaat his first victory over their ancient rivals. Celtic had to stop Rangers extending their lead to 13 points and hoped they could cut it to seven.

Dick Advocaat decided to leave Jorg Albertz on the bench, and instead used Neil McCann and Andrei Kanchelskis on the flanks. Celtic used a new formation with Jackie McNamara in central midfield and Vidar Riseth at full-back. It took time for the visitors to settle into their rhythm, but all the time Rangers had Celtic under pressure. Amoruso had a header cleared off the line by Lambert after four minutes, with Gould beaten, and while the Celtic keeper managed to get a hand to a Rod Wallace shot five minutes later, if the rebound had fallen more kindly for McCann, Rangers would have secured the opening goal. McCann had two more chances before Celtic started to move forward and posted a warning when Mahe hit the bar with a speculative cross.

Six minutes before half-time Celtic took the lead. McNamara fed Stubbs and he hit a shot which gave Klos no chance. Any pattern in the match had gone and was replaced with raw desire and it was that which brought about Rangers' equaliser on the stroke of half-time. McCann whipped in a cross and Gabriel Amato, who had missed so many chances in his first Old Firm match, flashed a header which blasted into the net. The Argentinian ripped off his jersey in an elaborate celebration – and was booked for his trouble.

Celtic threatened after the break, but it was Rangers who took the lead. Amato powered his way past two Celtic defenders, but when Boyd stopped him, the ball broke to Wallace, who drilled it into the net from 18 yards.

Rangers should have consolidated but slow reactions from Klos saw Celtic equalise. He watched as Lubomir Moravcik's 25-yard shot cannoned off his crossbar after 66 minutes. Henrik Larsson headed the rebound in off a post – even though Klos managed to get to his feet and have a slap at the ball.

Eight players were booked in a match peppered with the usual controversy. Celtic felt they should have had a penalty when Stubbs was brought down in the box, and Rangers thought the centre-half should have been sent off for a foul on Klos. But the grudges were even – just like the game.

Rod Wallace scored to put Rangers 2-1 up.

THE WINTER BREAK – RANGERS ON TOP

As Dick Advocaat prepared to take his squad to the sunshine of Miami for the winter break, he could be well pleased with how his Ibrox career had started. Rangers were four points clear of Kilmarnock at the top of the Scottish Premier League, and – significantly – ten points ahead of Celtic.

The Ibrox side had won the first trophy of the season, the Scottish League Cup, beating St Johnstone 2-1 in the final at Celtic Park. The team, full of new names, was gelling and had learned the winning habit. Rangers had got back to where the fans were used to seeing them – the top of the domestic game.

The change in direction which Rangers chairman David Murray had tried to embark upon when he brought in Advocaat had shown signs of success in other areas. Rangers wanted success in Europe and Advocaat was bringing a style of football to Ibrox which could be successful in continental competition. In their UEFA Cup run, the Ibrox side had shown that under Advocaat they were capable of making an impression. Having got past tricky draws against PAOK Salonika and Beitar Jerusalem, Rangers had achieved one of their best results ever in Europe by beating Bayer Leverkusen in Germany. Even in defeat to the eventual winners of the UEFA Cup, Parma, they had shown they could compete with Europe's best, and if they had had just a little more good fortune they could have beaten them and reached the quarter-finals at the Italians' expense. And all of this had been achieved in double quick time.

Not every one of Advocaat's new signings had been a success however, and for a number of reasons he had to go back into the transfer market to strengthen the squad. Daniel Prodan was to spend his first season in the treatment room at Ibrox trying to get over a knee injury. Lionel Charbonnier, having won over the hearts of the Rangers fans as Andy Goram's successor, injured a knee against Leverkusen and his season was finished. Advocaat bought Borussia Dortmund's goalkeeper Stefan Klos for £700,000 to take over in goal.

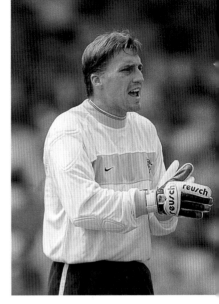

Klos was brought in from former German Champions Borussia Dortmund.

The teams swap shirts and players shake hands at the end of the tough Rangers vs. Bayer Leverkusen tie.

Ode To Joy: The Gers celebrate their 3-0 win over Hearts on October 17, 1998.

Up front, Gabriel Amato had struggled to make an impact and Rangers had bought French international Stephane Guivarc'h for £3.5 million from Newcastle United to help get the goals. He had an explosive start with two goals on his debut against St Johnstone, but by the winter break he still hadn't settled in properly. Rangers fans are used to continental stars signing at Ibrox, but Advocaat also showed his faith in Scottish talent by signing Neil McCann from Hearts for £1.5 million. He went on to prove himself one of the most significant signings of the season.

But if there was one problem that Advocaat was facing in terms of success, it was one that was very close to home. He had failed to taste victory in three attempts at the Old Firm derby against Celtic. Indeed it was worse than that. At Parkhead, he had faced the humiliation of a 5-1 defeat. That was one score which Rangers were already planning to settle as they took stock at the winter break. But the fixture congestion of the early part of the season had been successfully negotiated, and with matches better spaced out in the second half of the season, Advocaat could look forward to establishing a more even rhythm about his team's performances.

Jorg Albertz proudly lifts the League Cup.

RANGERS 2 0 STENHOUSEMUIR

match highlights

Tennents Scottish Cup
3rd Round 23 January 1999
Attendance: 37,759
Referee: M Clark (Edinburgh)

This game was more about Stenhousemuir enjoying a day out on the big stage than being any yardstick to measure Rangers against. The home side did their job and were never in any danger, but whatever the score it would have been difficult for them to emerge with much credit.

The most notable fact was probably that Stenhousemuir's veteran defender Graeme Armstrong was making his 1,000th senior appearance. Mind you, with Adrian Sprott – the man who scored Hamilton's notorious winner at Ibrox in the Cup in 1986 – in the side, there were bound to be some nerves and he did nothing to settle them when he hit Stefan Klos's post in the third minute.

But Rangers were in the lead just 60 seconds later, when Stephane Guivarc'h's shot hit a defender and went over Stenny keeper Lindsay Hamilton and into the net.

The expected goal flood didn't come, but Rangers put the game beyond the visitors seven minutes before half-time. Hamilton couldn't hold on to a stiff drive from Albertz, and as ever, Wallace was on hand to scamper in and finish off from close range.

Stenhousemuir had their moments up at the other end in the second half but Rangers ought to have increased their lead when they were awarded a penalty after Neil McCann was brought down by Alan Lawrence. Hamilton made a fine low save from Albertz's unusually inaccurate spot kick to deny Rangers, but the Ibrox side swept their way comfortably into the next round.

'Stenhousemuir made it very difficult. We can't plan for games like this but they gave us a tough test.'

— Dick Advocaat

RANGERS

Klos
Porrini
Wilson
Vidmar
Hendry
Kanchelskis
Albertz (Van Bronckhorst 61)
McCann (B Ferguson 78)
Miller
Guivarc'h 4 (Amato 61)
Wallace 38

substitutes
Amato
B Ferguson
Van Bronckhorst

STENHOUSEMUIR

L Hamilton
Davidson
Sprott (Banks 81)
Armstrong
Baptie
Gibson (Lansdowne 85)
R. Hamilton
Fisher
Lawrence
Craig
Miller (Watters 81)

substitutes
Banks
Lansdowne
Watters

Amato chips the ball but he can't stretch quite enough – it was not on target.

DUNDEE 0   4 RANGERS

Scottish Premier League
27 January 1999
Attendance: 9,453
Referee: J McCluskey (Stewarton)

DUNDEE

Douglas
Adamczuk
Irvine (Smith 56)
Anderson (Strachan 74)
Annand
Grady
Maddison
Falconer
Rae
Robertson (McSkimming 84)
Tweed

substitutes
McSkimming
Smith
Strachan

RANGERS

Klos
Porrini
Amoruso
Kanchelskis
Albertz
Guivarc'h 12 (Johansson 64)
Wallace
McCann
Nicholson
Vidmar
Miller 8, 43 (Feeney 78)

substitutes
Johansson 76
Feeney
Wilson

match highlights

At Dens park, Rangers began a sequence of three away matches which Dick Advocaat said he thought could decide the Championship. In a clinical performance, an understrength Rangers side destroyed a similarly-handicapped Dundee.

Without the suspended Colin Hendry, Giovanni van Bronckhorst and Barry Ferguson, the Rangers manager gave Charlie Miller only his second start of the season, and brought in reserve captain Barry Nicholson for his first team debut. Numan and Ian Ferguson were also missing due to injury.

After a lively start from Dundee, Rangers established a stranglehold on the game and took the lead after just eight minutes. Wallace broke through the Dundee rearguard and squared the ball to Miller who swept it past Douglas for the opener. Later, Kanchelskis was unlucky not to score with a volley, but Guivarc'h made it 2-0 after 12 minutes with a simple tap-in after good work from Albertz and McCann.

The match was over as a contest before it had really begun, and Rangers underlined that fact with a third goal two minutes before half-time. Kanchelskis danced his way past defenders down the right and fed Miller in the box. Showing a great deal of poise for a man just back in the team, Miller controlled the ball, made himself space and then slipped the ball past Douglas for his second goal.

In the second half, Rangers threatened to humiliate the home side with Kanchelskis in particular on rampant form, but they had to wait until 14 minutes before the end before they scored any more goals. Johansson, on for the injured Guivarc'h, was put through by Albertz and slipped the ball under Douglas from 12 yards for his tenth goal of the season. New signing from Linfield Lee Feeney made his first senior appearance coming on for Miller towards the end of a good night's work by Rangers.

Charlie Miller – in only his second start of the season – celebrates his second goal of the match.

ABERDEEN 2 4 RANGERS

match highlights

Scottish Premier League
30 January 1999
Attendance: 19,537
Referee: K Clark (Paisley)

Rangers did enough to win this game twice, but after a comeback from Aberdeen it took two late goals to finally clinch the victory. There was no doubt that Advocaat was sure what his best team is, because he dropped Charlie Miller to the bench, preferring Giovanni van Bronckhorst who had served his suspension.

The match started with a passion we have come to expect from an Aberdeen side which is always fired up when Rangers come to town, if no one else. Mike Newell was booked after just two minutes, but within 11 minutes the visitors were 2-0 up.

Van Bronckhorst floated in a free-kick towards the far post and Sergio Porrini flicked a header past Leighton. One minute later, Neil McCann broke free down the left and when he centred he found Wallace in space. The striker clipped the ball past Leighton for his 20th goal of the season and it looked as though Rangers were going to hand out another thrashing. But having lost at home to Second Division Livingston in the Scottish Cup the previous week, the Dons were desperate to make amends in front of their own fans. At first they were restricted to long-range efforts, but when Winters crossed into the box after 34 minutes, Newell was there to score with a diving header.

Five minutes after half-time and Aberdeen had scored a spectacular – if controversial – equaliser. Referee Kenny Clark decided Amoruso had passed the ball back to Klos in his own penalty area. Dow touched the free-kick back to Jess who thundered a drive high into the net from 20 yards. Eight minutes later Scott Wilson was sent off for the second time this season for a second bookable offence on Winters.

With four minutes left it looked as though Rangers had dropped two points, but they came storming back. Kanchelskis surged into the penalty area and was brought down by John Inglis. Albertz took the spot-kick and Rangers were 3-2 up. Rangers made it four in the last minute. Van Bronckhorst got past two defenders, slipped the ball to Albertz, and the German passed on to Kanchelskis, allowing the winger to roll the ball into an empty net.

ABERDEEN

Leighton
Perry
Whyte
Inglis
Smith
Jess 50
Newell 34
Mayer
Kiriakov (Dow 45)
Young
Winters

substitutes
Dow

RANGERS

Klos
Porrini 10
Amoruso
Kanchelskis 90
Van Bronckhorst
Albertz 86 (pen) (Miller 90)
Guivarc'h (Nicholson 60)
Wallace 11
McCann (Johansson 77)
Wilson
Vidmar

substitutes
Nicholson
Johansson
Miller

Andrei Kanchelskis, scorer of goal number four, is congratulated by the Rangers crowd.

DUNFERMLINE 0   3 RANGERS

Scottish Premier League
7 February 1999
Attendance: 11,500
Referee: W Young (Clarkston)

DUNFERMLINE

Butler
Shields
Tod
French
Huxford
Smith
Johnson
Shaw
Graham
D Ferguson
McGroaty (Nish 74)

substitutes
Nish
Westwater
Fraser
McDonald

RANGERS

Klos
Porrini
Amoruso
Ferguson
Kanchelskis 56
Van Bronckhorst
Albertz
Wallace
Johansson 59, 90
Nicholson (McCann 45)
Vidmar

substitutes
McCann
Miller
Guivarc'h

match highlights

East End Park on a cold February night is not one of the glamour ties of Scottish football, but Rangers secured three valuable points there to end their sequence of away matches with a maximum nine points out of nine. Rangers brought in Barry Nicholson for the suspended Scott Wilson, welcomed back Barry Ferguson and started with Johansson rather than Guivarc'h up front.

Dunfermline were desperate for the points and matched Rangers stride for stride in the first half. Both sides had chances as the Pars showed they were not overawed by taking on the League leaders. David Graham had a shot blocked by Klos and just before the break a rocket from Albertz swerved narrowly wide.

Rangers reorganised at half-time. McCann came on for Nicholson, with Vidmar moving to right-back and van Bronckhorst dropping deep on the left. Dunfermline started the second half brightly and twice tested Klos, but it was Rangers who made the breakthrough after 56 minutes with a breathtaking goal. Wallace pumped in a deep cross from the left and Kanchelskis launched a full-blooded right foot volley which flew into the net. The first goal was crucial and three minutes later Rangers scored their second. McCann picked out Johansson on the edge of the box, and the Finn swivelled round before firing a fierce left-foot drive past Butler.

Dunfermline should have clawed their way back when they were awarded a controversial penalty, after Kanchelskis was adjudged to have pushed Colin Nish in the box, but justice was done when Andy Smith blasted the spot-kick wide.

Dunfermline then went for broke with four men up front, but Rangers stepped up the tempo. It brought rewards right on the final whistle when Johansson got his second with a tap-in after good work from Wallace.

Andrei Kanchelskis scored with a stunning right-foot volley to give Rangers the lead.

HAMILTON 0 6 RANGERS

match highlights

Tennents Scottish Cup
4th Round 14 February 1999
Attendance: 7,339
Referee: M McCurry (Glasgow)

Rangers reached the quarter-finals of the Scottish Cup with a 6-0 demolition of Hamilton in which they were never required to break sweat. It took just four minutes on a wet night at Firhill to dismiss any suggestions of an upset. A van Bronckhorst corner from the right was flicked on by Albertz to Johansson. His header was at first blocked by Renicks, but the rebound fell to the Finn's feet and he rifled it into the net.

Rangers seemed almost bored by this game, but they increased their lead three minutes before half-time with a penalty. Neil McCann went on a solo run down the left and cut inside rather than passing. Hillcoat sprinted off his line, and although McCann had pushed the ball too far in front of himself, the keeper brought him down. Albertz sent him the wrong way from the spot for Rangers' second.

In the second half Rangers woke up, and with Kanchelskis rediscovering his appetite for the game, they laid waste to Hamilton in a 19-minute spell. Rangers forced a pair of corners after Hillcoat turned a Johansson shot behind, and from the second, van Bronckhorst found Vidmar who headed in for his first goal of the season. In the 65th minute Kanchelskis darted down the right, cut inside and, after a one-two with Miller, rifled the ball into the net for Rangers' fourth. Johansson got his second after Guivarc'h played a ball from Kanchelskis into his path for the fifth, and McCann scored his first goal for Rangers with 15 minutes to go with a right foot shot to make it six.

HAMILTON

J Hillcoat
Renicks
Cunnington
C Hillcoat
Berry
Thomson
McAulay (McKenzie 68)
N.Henderson (Moore 62)
McCormick
Wales
D Henderson (Clark 68)

substitutes
Clark
McKenzie
Moore

RANGERS

Klos
Porrini
Amoruso
Vidmar 56 (Wilson 81)
Ferguson
Van Bronckhorst
Kanchelskis 65
McCann 75
Albertz 42 (pen) (Miller 62)
Wallace (Guivarc'h 45)
Johansson 4, 72

substitutes
Guivarc'h
Miller
Wilson

Kanchelskis was again involved in the goalmouth action. This time he scored Rangers' fourth goal.

RANGERS 6   1 DUNDEE

Scottish Premier League
20 February 1999
Attendance: 49,462
Referee: D Smith (Troon)

RANGERS

Klos
Porrini
Amoruso
Vidmar
Kanchelskis
Ferguson (Miller 71)
Van Bronckhorst 88
Albertz 24 (pen), 38, 57
McCann 51, 71
Wallace (Amato 77)
Johansson (Guivarc'h 57)

substitutes
Amato
Guivarc'h
Miller

DUNDEE

Douglas
Adamczuk 28 (Rae 77)
Smith
Tweed
Rogers
Maddison
Falconer
Strachan
McSkimming
Coyne (Annand 63)
Grady

substitutes
Annand
Rae
Sharp

match highlights

This was a Rangers team at their most devastating. It can take time for a team to gel, but everything clicked for the Ibrox side as they swept Dundee United aside with six sparkling goals.

The Dens Park side came to defend and played with only one striker up front. That allowed Dick Advocaat to switch to a 3-5-2 formation and his players certainly responded well to the opportunity. Jorg Albertz did more than most. His place in the team had not been certain, but he worked tirelessly and was rewarded with a hat-trick. Rangers appeared to stutter when Adamczuk levelled Albertz's opening goal in the 28th minute, but the German restored the home side's lead ten minutes later and in the second half Rangers were irresistible and totally dominated the game.

Andrei Kanchelskis had possibly his best game in a Rangers jersey, beating men and whipping in dangerous crosses, while van Bronckhorst was at his creative best. He capped his display with a goal two minutes from time, but by then Albertz had completed his hat-trick and the pace of McCann had been rewarded with a brace of goals.

Those hoping for Rangers to stumble – an thereby open up the title race – seemed destined to be disappointed by this result, as Advocaat's team took another significant step to regaining the title.

Neil McCann slips the ball into the back of the net as Douglas can only look on helplessly.

KILMARNOCK 0 5 RANGERS

match highlights

Scottish Premier League
28 February 1999
Attendance: 16,242
Referee: S Dougal (Glasgow)

Playing Kilmarnock at Rugby Park was always going to be a severe test, but it was one which Rangers passed with flying colours. They were simply a class above the opposition. In fact, if they had kept up their momentum, the League leaders could have scored a lot more than five goals. They took the lead after just five minutes, and it was fitting that Andrei Kanchelskis and Neil McCann combined for the Scot to score – the two wingers ran the show for the visitors.

Rangers didn't add to their score until a devastating last 15 minutes, but the assurance of their performance meant that no one doubted the result. Former Ranger Ally McCoist came closest to an equaliser midway through the second half, but that only served to spur the Ibrox side into action. McCann stole the ball off the toe of Ally Mitchell, hit the by-line and his cut-back was met perfectly by Rod Wallace for the killer second goal after 75 minutes. Johansson got the third ten minutes later, and then Wallace got his second and Rangers' 100th goal of the season with a brilliant header after being set up by van Bronckhorst. The fifth goal capped a marvellous night for Wallace, when a shot was blocked and he was there to snap up the rebound and clip it into the net.

Three more points for Rangers, with a result which must have sapped the resolve of the others in the title chase; surely only champions got to a place like Kilmarnock and scored five goals.

KILMARNOCK

Marshall
Hamilton (Mitchell 73)
Montgomerie
McGowne
Baker
Holt
Reilly
Durrant
Burke
McCoist (Roberts 83)
Wright

substitutes
Mitchell
Roberts
Mahood

RANGERS

Klos
Porrini (Nicholson 83)
Amoruso
Vidmar
Kanchelskis
Ferguson
Van Bronckhorst
Albertz (Hendry 70)
McCann 5
Guivarc'h (Johansson 80)
Wallace 75, 87, 90

substitutes
Hendry
Johansson 85
Nicholson

McCann and Kanchelskis celebrate the important opening goal.

RANGERS 2   1 FALKIRK

Tennents Scottish Cup
Quarter-final 6 March 1999
Attendance: 39,250
Referee: J Rowbotham (Kirkcaldy)

RANGERS

Klos
Porrini
Amoruso 75
Vidmar (Amato 66)
Ferguson
Kanchelskis
Van Bronckhorst
Albertz
Guivarc'h (Johansson 50)
Wallace
McCann 52 (Wilson 85)

substitutes
Amato
Johansson
Wilson

FALKIRK

Mathers
Corrigan
McQuilken
Sinclair
James
Den Bieman
McAllister
Keith
Crabbe
Moss 59
McKenzie

substitutes
McCart
Hutchinson
Seaton

match highlights

It took an inspirational strike from Rangers captain Lorenzo Amoruso to get past a Falkirk side which refused to lie down.

The home side failed to fire on all cylinders, while the visitors – who have a fine Cup record – looked determined to claim another big-name scalp on a ground where they have played well in recent seasons. They beat Celtic at Ibrox in the Cup semi-final in 1997.

Falkirk had the first chance when Klos could only punch out a Scott Crabbe corner, but Sinclair hit the rebound over the bar. At the other end, Paul Mathers was in tremendous form and pulled off good saves to deny first Wallace and then Guivarc'h.

Falkirk were doing a good job of holding Rangers and then hitting them on the break, and they were unlucky to go one down seven minutes after half-time. Van Bronckhorst swung in a corner and Neil McCann ghosted in, in front of Mathers, to head the ball into the net. The game opened up and first Crabbe hit the woodwork, before Albertz did the same at the other end. Seven minutes later, tenacious Falkirk levelled the match. Keith saw his shot blocked, but Moss was on hand to fire the rebound into the net.

Rangers surged forward but couldn't break down the Bairns defence. It need a moment of inspiration and Amoruso provided it. The Rangers captain strode forward into the Falkirk half, and his swerving shot from 30 yards bounced in front of Mathers before going in at his right-hand post.

'It was a poor performance. Our attitude was a problem.'

— DICK ADVOCAAT

McCann again: congratulated by captain Amoruso for his second-half goal.

RANGERS 2   1 MOTHERWELL

match highlights

Scottish Premier League
13 March 1999
Attendance: 49,483
Referee: B Orr (Kilbarchan)

Rangers recorded their ninth win in a row, but in the end they made life a lot more difficult for themselves than it ought to have been. On a day when Andy Goram made an emotional return to Ibrox in Motherwell colours, a combination of The Goalie's brilliance at restricting his former side to just two goals, and a bit of complacency, led to a nervous finish.

    Rod Wallace had the ball in the net within a minute only for the 'goal' to be disallowed for offside. It set the tone for a first half which Rangers dominated. Jonatan Johansson missed two good chances in the first ten minutes, and Neil McCann saw a first-time volley beat Goram but whistle past the post. After 28 minutes a tremendous volley from van Bronckhorst took a deflection off Wallace, but Goram made a marvellous reflex save. Three minutes later Goram was beaten. Van Bronckhorst found Kanchelskis with a 60-yard pass and he crossed for Wallace. The ball flew in for his 24th goal of the season.

But a one-goal lead was not a good return for Rangers' efforts in the first half. After the break both McCann and Johansson went close as Rangers tried to kill off the game. In the 59th minute it was the Finn who got the breakthrough. After a succession of corners, Albertz whipped one in, Porrini headed down and when Goram parried the ball, Johansson was there to tap it into the net for his seventh goal in eight games. But Rangers made the mistake of thinking it was all over. Substitute Pat Nevin broke free on the right, and when he crossed, Barry Ferguson failed to pick up debutant Mike Gower, who headed into the net.

The final 20 minutes were filled with anxiety with Rangers not sure whether to risk going for a third, or to hold on. In the final minutes they were nearly punished for their indecision when Michael Doesburg got free in the box, but he couldn't find the net.

Jonaton Johansson scored Rangers' second goal just before his team conceded one at the other end.

RANGERS

Klos
Porrini
Amoruso
Vidmar
Kanchelskis (Miller 86)
Ferguson (McInnes 76)
Albertz
Van Bronckhorst
McCann (Amato 90)
Wallace 31
Johansson 59

substitutes
McInnes
Miller
Amato

MOTHERWELL

Goram
May
Teale
McGowan
McMillan
Brannan
Valakari
Doesburg
Gower 68 (Matthaei 86)
McCulloch (Miller 76)
Adams (Nevin 65)

substitutes
Nevin
Miller
Matthaei

RANGERS 0 1 DUNDEE UNITED

Scottish Premier League
20 March 1999
Attendance: 49,164
Referee: M Clark (Edinburgh)

RANGERS

Klos
Porrini
Amoruso
Wilson (Amato 45)
Vidmar (Miller 74)
Kanchelskis
Van Bronckhorst
Albertz
McCann
Wallace
Johansson

substitutes
Amato
Miller
McInnes
Nicholson

DUNDEE UNITED

Dijkstra
Jonsson
Duffy
De Vos
Skoldmark
McCullock
Easton
Hannah
Eustace (Patterson 74)
Dodds
Olofsson 44 (Mathie 83)

substitutes
Mathie
Patterson
Miller

match highlights

Rangers had won games without playing very well in previous weeks – this time they got the result which their play deserved.

The Ibrox side were slack at the back, and despite creating a number of chances, there was no one up front willing to take responsibility. United were in desperate need of a win, and Paul Sturrock's well-organised side did a good job of containing the League leaders, and got the break they needed up front. In the first ten minutes Rangers created three gilt-edged chances but missed them all.

For ten minutes before half-time, United gradually crept forward. They held the upper hand in midfield, and their pressure was rewarded with a goal. In the 44th minute John Eustace slipped the ball through a stationary Rangers defence and Kjell Olofsson bulleted it into the net. The opening goal was the key to the match, and from then on United stuck to their task of closing down Rangers and getting as many men as possible behind the ball. Rangers showed more urgency in the second half, but with United slamming the door firmly at the back, the home side had no luck in front of goal. Even when United were reduced to ten men, Rangers could not press home their advantage, which had by that time become significant. There just wasn't enough variety up front to get the breakthrough. This was the first time Dick Advocaat had experienced losing at Ibrox.

Dijkstra lies helpless as Amato and Johansson struggle to control the ball in a fruitless goalmouth tangle.

ST JOHNSTONE 3 1 RANGERS

match highlights

Scottish Premier League
4 April 1999
Attendance: 9,740
Referee: H Dallas (Motherwell)

After losing to Dundee United two weeks earlier, Rangers were expected to roar back at Perth. Instead they whimpered, as St Johnstone took another three points off the Championship challengers.

This may have been thought to be a dress rehearsal for the meeting of the two sides in the Scottish Cup just one week later, but the Saints held nothing back as Rangers failed to fire. The defence, too, was a shambles and St Johnstone's first two goals came from free-kicks needlessly given away by Lorenzo Amoruso and Tony Vidmar.

Jim Weir's first-half goal was equalled by Craig Moore's after 58 minutes, but Rangers never really looked as if they would take anything from this match. The midfield wasn't much more organised than the rearguard, giving away possession of the ball far too easily. Out of the entire team, Dick Advocaat could have spared only Rod Wallace from scathing criticsm. The English striker was tireless in his running and held on to the ball well, but where he led no one else followed.

Added to the home defeat by Dundee United a week earlier, this result made it look as though the title race was going to go to the wire, as Rangers failed to take the chance to open up a nine-point gap over Celtic. The message was clear: Rangers needed to rediscover the resolve and creativity of earlier in the season, and make sure this blip didn't turn into a major slump.

ST JOHNSTONE

Main
Weir 14
Kernaghan
Dods
Bollan
McAnespie 90
O'Halloran (Griffin 80)
Dasovic
Kane
McBride (Simao 58)
Grant (Lowndes 82)

substitutes
Griffin
Lowndes
Simao 73
Preston
Ferguson

RANGERS

Klos
Porrini
Moore 58
Amoruso
Vidmar (Amato 70)
Kanchelskis
Van Bronckhorst
Wallace
Johansson
Albertz
McCann

substitute
Amato
McInnes
Wilson

Craig Moore watches his header bounce over the line to equalise for Rangers.

RANGERS 4   0 ST JOHNSTONE

Tennents Scottish Cup
Semi-final 11 April 1999
Attendance: 20,664
Referee: J McCluskey (Stewarton)

RANGERS

Klos
Porrini
Amoruso
Kanchelskis (McInnes 71)
Van Bronckhorst 33
Albertz
Guivarc'h (Johansson 56)
Wallace 15
McCann 70
Vidmar
Hendry (Wilson 76)

substitutes
Johansson 62
McInnes
Wilson

ST JOHNSTONE

Main
Dasovic (Griffin 73)
Weir
Kernaghan
Grant (Lowndes 65)
Kane
Bollan
O'Halloran
McBride (Simao 22)
McAnespie
Dods

substitutes
Griffin
Lowndes
Simao

match highlights

Rangers were still smarting from their 3-1 defeat by St Johnstone the week before which had dented, but not really damaged, their title chances. They were in no mood to let the Perth side deny them their chance in the Cup – and the treble dream.

The Rangers side looked completely different and dominated this semi-final from start to finish. Strengthened by the return of Colin Hendry, who had been missing since January, they took the lead after 15 minutes and never looked back.

Van Bronckhorst found McCann in space on the left, Wallace made a run from deep, and when the winger lofted the ball into his path, he tucked it past Main. A well-rehearsed free-kick brought Rangers' second. The Saints defence expected a blaster from Albertz, but instead he exchanged short passes with van Bronckhorst who smashed a shot into the net from the edge of the box.

Albertz rattled the cross bar with a 30-yard effort just before half-time, but Rangers didn't add to their score until the second half. After a period of sustained pressure, Albertz swung in a corner, Main flapped and completely lost it and Johansson was there at the far post to score his 17th goal of the season.

The German was also involved in the build-up for the fourth when he combined well with Kanchelskis to feed McCann who drove the ball into the net. St Johnstone had felt the full wrath of a rampant Rangers side.

Jonaton Johansson celebrates Rangers' third goal – there was another to follow.

RANGERS 1   0 DUNFERMLINE

match highlights

Scottish Premier League
14 April 1999
Attendance: 46,220
Referee: W Young (Clarkston)

This was three points ground out in the push for the Championship, as Dunfermline desperately tried to get a point in their battle against the drop.

Rangers had by far the bulk of the possession, with Andrei Kanchelskis and Neil McCann rampant down the flanks. Unfortunately the Ibrox side could create few clear-cut chances to take advantage of their dominance, and Dunfermline were always threatening on the break. After two League defeats in a row, Rangers had got back on track against St Johnstone in the Cup semi-final but three League points were vital and in those circumstances it was a good result. But Dunfermline almost took the lead in the very first minute. Amoruso was dispossessed by former Ranger David Graham, but his defensive partner Colin Hendry rushed back to charge down the shot. That was the first of four chances for the visitors which tested the home nerves. The warning was heeded and Rangers sprang forward. Kanchelskis went on a run and when his shot was blocked by Lee Butler, the Ibrox side forced four corners in three minutes.

Rangers were unlucky after a quarter of an hour when Guivarc'h hit the bar, but Scott Thompson almost came as close with a 30-yard drive which flashed past Klos's left-hand post. Moments later Rangers scored the goal which settled their nerves and the match. Kanchelskis broke down the right, found Giovanni van Bronckhorst with a pass and the Dutchman cut across the penalty area before burying a 20-yard drive low into the net.

Both Kanchelskis and Guivarc'h had chances to increase Rangers' lead before the break, but by that time the tempo had cooled. The home side squandered a number of half-chances and the closest they came to increasing their lead was when Hendry hit the bar with a header. Six games to go in the run-in to the Championship and Rangers were getting the right results, even if their performances lacked punch.

RANGERS

Klos
Porrini
Amoruso
Vidmar
Hendry
Kanchelskis
Van Bronckhorst 37
Albertz
Guivarc'h (Johansson 75)
Wallace
McCann

substitutes
Johansson
Amato
McInnes

DUNFERMLINE

Butler
Shields
Coyle
Tod
Millar
Huxford
Petrie
Thomson
Graham
Dair
Dolan

substitutes
Smith
Squires
Westwater

Van Bronckhorst scores the winning goal with a superb drive from just outside the penalty area.

DUNDEE 1   1 RANGERS

Scottish Premier League
17 April 1999
Attendance: 11,051
Referee: J Rowbotham (Kirkcaldy)

DUNDEE

Douglas
Smith
Irvine
Anderson 23
Grady
Maddison
Coyne (Falconer 73)
McSkimming
Miller
Rae
Boyack

substitutes
Falconer
McInally
Strachan

RANGERS

Klos
Porrini
Amoruso
Kanchelskis (Hendry 79)
Van Bronckhorst
Albertz
Wallace
McCann
Johansson (Amato 65)
Vidmar 49
Reyna (McInnes 80)

substitutes
Amato
Hendry
McInnes

match highlights

Rangers' waltz towards the title was knocked out of its stride by Dundee's best and most determined performance of the season. The match was played at Tannadice, as building work started on Dens Park, but Dundee seemed perfectly at home.

The fact they didn't manage to take all three points was a tribute to Rangers' resilience when faced by a team on fire. It was two former Rangers who combined to give the Dark Blues the lead after 23 minutes. Steven Boyack broke down the right after a superb crossfield pass from McSkimming and the winger delivered a superb cross into the area. Little Iain Anderson rose above Porrini, met the cross and powered a header past Klos.

Dundee had the bit between their teeth and with Rab Douglas in superb form at the other end, Rangers could find no way through. Just before half-time he brilliantly parried a Wallace shot before getting off the ground to clear as Johansson tried to snap up the rebound. Seconds later he had luck on his side when Johansson headed wide.

Rangers roared into action at the start of the second half, and Albertz came close with a shot one minute into it. Two minutes later the German created the opening from which Rangers got the equaliser, swinging in a corner which Vidmar powered in with his head. The scene was set for Rangers to overwhelm Dundee, but instead it was the home side who created a number of second-half chances they just couldn't convert. In the end it was a point won for Rangers rather than two lost.

Goalkeeper Rab Douglas put on a superb performance to deny Rangers the goals they so keenly sought.

RANGERS 3 1 ABERDEEN

match highlights

Scottish Premier League
25 April 1999
Attendance: 49,145
Referee: M McCurry (Glasgow)

With Celtic's title challenge disintegrating the day before with a 1-0 defeat at St Johnstone, Rangers set up the chance to win the title at Parkhead with a satisfying 3-1 victory over Aberdeen.

In the first half, though, the Dons made them fight for it and took the lead after creating a couple of good openings. Eoin Jess was almost back to his best and was unfortunate not to score with a scorching right-foot drive from 25 yards which rattled the bar. Rangers still hadn't got over the shock of that when they went 0-1 down after 20 minutes. Jess found Jim Hamilton on the right, and when he crossed, Mark Perry was standing unmarked on the six yard line. The Dons defender couldn't miss – and he didn't.

Aberdeen had a penalty claim turned down, and then Rangers went about the business of gaining control of the match. In the 26th minute it was the home side who were awarded a penalty when Wallace was barged in the back by Whyte. Amato scored from the spot. That settled Rangers but they had to wait until the second half before they took the lead as Aberdeen's challenge withered.

Kanchelskis cut in from the right and when he reached the 18 yard line he fired in a shot which deflected off Whyte's chest to scream past keeper Warner and go low into the net. Four minutes later and Rangers scored a third – but there was no luck about this one, just quality. Amato slipped the ball through to Wallace and as Warner came off his line, the Englishman delicately dinked it over him and into the net.

RANGERS

Klos
Porrini
Amoruso
Hendry
Nicholson (McInnes 46)
Kanchelskis 55
▮ Van Bronckhorst
Amato 27 (pen) (Johansson 78)
Wallace 60
McCann
Reyna

substitutes
McInnes
Johansson
Guivarc'h

ABERDEEN

Warner
Perry 19
Whyte
Smith
Hamilton
Jess
Mayer
Dow
Bernard
▮ Young
Winters

substitutes
Leighton
Anderson
Buchan

Rod Wallace is brought down in the area. Rangers equalised when the penalty was converted by Amato.

CELTIC 0   3 RANGERS

Scottish Premier League
2 May 1999
Attendance: 59,918
Referee: H Dallas (Motherwell)

CELTIC

Kerr ▧
Annoni ▧
Marshall
Stubbs ▧
Riseth ▧ ▨
Mahe ▧ ▧
Lambert
Wieghorst ▧ (Healy 69)
Larsson
Viduka
Brattbakk (Donnelly 60)

substitutes
Donnelly
Healy ▧
Johnson

RANGERS

Klos
Porrini
Amoruso
Vidmar ▧
Hendry
Van Bronckhorst
Albertz 44 (pen) (McInnes 85)
McCann 12, 76 ▧
Reyna
Wallace ▨
Amato ▧ (Johansson 73)

substitutes
Johansson
McInnes
Niemi

match highlights

Dick Advocaat tasted victory in an Old Firm fixture for the first time, as Rangers clinched the title at Parkhead for the first time.

But for many the memory of this match will bring back a bitter taste as sectarian hatred marred what should have been a showcase occasion. Rangers got off to a marvellous start when they took the lead in a lightning attack after 12 minutes. Van Bronckhorst prodded the ball to Wallace on the left and he bore into the box. The striker flashed the ball into the path of McCann making a late run and he crashed the ball into the net.

That settled Rangers' nerves, but shattered the composure of more than one Celtic player. Stephane Mahe, who had been booked early in the match, lost the plot when Neil McCann fouled him in the 31st minute. Referee Hugh Dallas gave the free-kick, but before he could do anything else, Mahe made threatening gestures to McCann and demanded, with full Gallic histrionics, that Dallas book the Rangers player. Dallas had no option but to send the Frenchman off, but at first he refused to go. The atmosphere had turned ugly even by Old Firm standards, and it was to get worse.

Rangers were awarded a free-kick on the right a few minutes later, and fans started breaching the security cordon and running onto the pitch trying to get at Dallas. Thankfully the security guards restrained each one in time, but they couldn't stop a coin thrown from the stands hitting the referee on the head. Dallas crouched down as blood poured from his headwound. When what passed for order was restored, the free kick was swung into the box and Riseth appeared to push Tony Vidmar out of the way. Dallas immediately awarded a penalty. As all around him seemed to be losing their heads, Jorg Albertz kept his and scored from the spot.

McCann scored again in the second half when he ran onto a Johansson pass and rounded Kerr before passing the ball into the net, but once the match was over as a contest, the discipline went on both sides. Dallas was frequently reaching into his pocket, Wallace and Riseth were sent off, leaving only 19 players on the pitch at the end.

Rangers won the title at Celtic's ground for the first time in their history.

That didn't stop Rangers celebrating at the end and the tears in Bert van Lingen's eyes as Dick Advocaat punched the air showed just what this first title meant to them. The only shame was that their hard-worked-for day of celebration was spoiled by others.

RANGERS 0 0 HEARTS

match highlights

Scottish Premier League
9 May 1999
Attendance: 49,495
Referee: S Dougal (Burnside)

Rangers celebrated winning the Championship after a long, hard season – even if there was little worth remembering in a dour 90 minutes. Perhaps after the events at Celtic Park the week before they were glad it was a dull affair. The most notable events in this pre-party match were two penalties – both missed by Rangers.

With nothing at stake for either side the match was played at a subdued tempo as the fans prepared for the presentation of the new SPL trophy. Hearts had chances to spoil the atmosphere when Adam set up Jackson after four minutes, but the former Celtic striker could only drive wide. With Rangers' killer instinct missing, the visitors had another opportunity just before the break when Adam tested Klos with a powerful header but the game sauntered to the interval without a goal. Andrei Kanchelskis tried to get enthusiastic in the second half, and when van Bronckhorst carved out an opening for him, the winger's shot was well saved by Rousset.

Then there was the saga of the penalties. It seemed a harsh decision after 53 minutes when Johansson lost his footing after Murray had shepherded the ball to safety and referee Stuart Dougal pointed to the spot. Perhaps Jorg Albertz felt it unfair, because he hit his spot-kick without conviction and Rousset saved it with his legs.

Seventeen minutes later and Rangers were awarded a stonewall penalty when Ritchie upended Amato. But the Argentinian fared no better than Albertz and sliced his kick well wide.

No matter. The Rangers fans were there to party, and as the Rangers captain Lorenzo Amoruso lifted the Championship trophy for the first time, the celebrations got under way.

RANGERS

Klos
Porrini
Amoruso
Wilson
Vidmar (Johansson 25)
Kanchelskis (McInnes 72)
Van Bronckhorst
Amato
Albertz
▌ McCann
Reyna

substitutes
Johansson
▌ McInnes
Niemi

HEARTS

Rousset
Naysmith
Ritchie
Adam
Cameron
▌ Jackson
Locke
▌ Pressley
Murray
Severin
McSwegan

substitutes
McPherson
McKenzie
Kirk

Neither team wanted to lose this match, and neither could do enough to win it.

MOTHERWELL 0   5 RANGERS

Scottish Premier League
15 May 1999
Attendance: 11,078
Referee: D Mcdonald (Edinburgh)

MOTHERWELL

Goram
Brannan
McGowan
Craigen
Gower (Ramsey 59)
Valakari
Spencer
McMillan
Goodman (Nicholas 45)
Adams (Nevin 59)
McCulloch ▮

substitutes
Nicholas 74
Nevin
Ramsey

RANGERS

Klos
Porrini
Amoruso
Wilson
Kanchelskis 65
Van Bronckhorst 37 (McInnes 65)
Reyna
Albertz
McCann (Johansson 65)
Amato 16, 51, 54 (pen)
Wallace

substitutes
McInnes
Johansson
Nicholson

match highlights

Rangers gained sweet revenge for their 1-0 defeat at Fir Park earlier in the season, banging in five goals despite facing former Rangers keeper Andy Goram in inspired form. Motherwell had been full of spirit when they won in October but they were a shadow of that team on this occasion.

Andy Goram (background) shows his frustration at being terrorised by Kanchelskis and Rangers.

Goram had no chance with any of the goals, but produced three stunning saves – from Giovanni van Bronckhorst, Jorg Albertz and Jonatan Johansson – to stop the rout becoming a total humiliation. Jamie McGowan misjudged a Claudio Reyna cross and Stephen Craigan lost Gabriel Amato, who had time to chest the ball down before sidefooting home from 15 yards. Van Bronckhorst notched the second, spectacularly volleying into Goram's top right-hand corner following a clever lay-off from Rod Wallace.

Amato's second strike was the pick of the afternoon. Collecting a headed pass from Wallace, he ran 40 yards and left three defenders in his wake before swerving past Goram and stroking the ball into the unguarded net. He completed his hat-trick from the penalty spot following McGowan's rash challenge on Wallace.

The rout was completed when Stephen McMillan failed to control Amato's through-ball and Andrei Kanchelskis, who had up until then had one of his more frustrating matches, lashed the loose ball behind Goram.

RANGERS 1 1 KILMARNOCK

match highlights

Scottish Premier League
23 May 1999
Attendance: 48,835
Referee: W Young (Clarkston)

Rangers were preparing for the following week's Scottish Cup Final while Kilmarnock needed a win to clinch a place in the UEFA Cup through their League placing. But while the Ayrshire side may have had more desire, they didn't have the quality to get the result they needed at Ibrox.

After just five minutes, Johansson lobbed the ball in from the left and Amato got his head to it, just evading the despairing grasp of Marshall in the Kilmarnock goal. But in a match of few chances, Killie, led by former Ranger Iain Durrant, regrouped and clawed their way back with an equaliser four minutes before half-time. Durrant flicked a clever cross into the box, and defender Kevin McGowne – supporting in attack – glanced a header past Klos.

Johansson and Vidmar didn't re-appear after the break and were replaced by McCann and McInnes in what was clearly a move to improve their fitness ahead of the Cup Final. Despite their need for a win, Kilmarnock lacked impetus, and with the Rangers players' minds on other things the momentum drifted from the match.

It staggered to a conclusion with few moments of note, except the sadness of the Killie players as their heads dropped at the end. Ten days later though, they were to hear they had qualified for the UEFA Cup through the Fair Play League.

For Rangers, it was the end of a long and successful campaign – but with one more match to play and one more prize to be won.

RANGERS

Klos
Porrini
Amoruso
Hendry (McCann 45)
Vidmar
Kanchelskis
Van Bronckhorst
Johansson
Reyna (McInnes 45)
Amato 5
Albertz

substitutes
McInnes
McCann
Wilson

KILMARNOCK

Marshall
MacPherson
Kerr
McGowne 41
Henry
Holt
Durrant
Mitchell
Mahood
Roberts (Vareille 45)
Lauchlan

substitutes
Vareille
Reilly
Meldrum

Amato tries to untangle himself from a brace of Kilmarnock players.

**Tennents Scottish Cup
Final 29 May 1998
Attendance: 52,000
Referee: H Dallas (Motherwell)**

RANGERS

Klos
Porrini (Kanchelskis 77)
Hendry
Amoruso
Vidmar
McCann (I Ferguson 67)
McInnes
Van Bronckhorst
Wallace 49
Amato (Wilson 90)
Albertz

substitutes
I Ferguson
Kanchelskis
Wilson

Scottish Cup Final

Dick Advocaat delivered the treble in his first season, with another victory over Celtic. The 1999 Scottish Cup Final was not a classic, but once again Rangers beat their oldest rivals when it mattered – and thankfully the horrific scenes of the League decider a couple of weeks earlier were not repeated. Appropriately the winner was scored by Rod Wallace. Signing the former Leeds striker under freedom of contract was arguably the best piece of business that Advocaat did all season, and Wallace's 27th goal of the season was enough to take the Scottish Cup to Ibrox and complete the sixth treble in Rangers' history. Four minutes after half-time in a match which was rarely inspiring, Wallace struck the winner.

Neil McCann weaves his way through three Celtic players.

The support from the loyal Rangers crowd was louder than ever for this monumental match.

The move started on the halfway line, when van Bronckhorst and surprise selection Derek McInnes combined well to release Tony Vidmar down the wing. The left-back made it to the bye-line and cut back into the box. Neil McCann went to snap up the ball, but when he was challenged by Alan Stubbs the ball fell to Wallace only a few yards out and he lifted his shot over Gould and into the net.

That left Celtic chasing the game, but with chances few and far between they rarely threatened. The Rangers defence dealt comfortably with their makeshift forward line of Lubomir Moravcik and a subdued Henrik Larsson. McCann and Wallace both had half-chances in the first half which were smothered by Gould, while in the 21st minute Paul Lambert came closest to scoring for Celtic with a shot which hit the bar.

But in a match marked by caution for both sides, once Wallace had struck, the Cup seemed destined for Ibrox. Celtic did have a penalty claim in the last few minutes when Amoruso blocked a Lambert shot, but TV evidence proved that the defender had used his chest and not a hand. Hugh Dallas called it correctly and waved away the protests from the Celtic players.

0 CELTIC

match highlights

Tennents Scottish Cup
Final 29 May 1998
Attendance: 52,000
Referee: H. Dallas (Motherwell)

All Over: The team celebrates their third and final trophy of the season. Two were won against Celtic.

CELTIC

Gould
Boyd
Mahe (O'Donnell 79)
Stubbs
Larsson
Wieghorst
Lambert
Annoni (Johnson 61)
Blinker
Moravcik
Mjallby

substitutes
Johnson
O'Donnell
Kerr

After an uncharacteristically barren season the year before, Rangers had swept all before them domestically and won everything. The players threw Dick Advocaat into the air as they celebrated at the end, and the Rangers manager revealed more reasons to be cheerful when they were finished – he had signed a two-year extension to his contract.

Goalmouth Action: Amato comes close to scoring as the action hots up in the Celtic goal.

SEASON REVIEW

Rangers chairman David Murray said at the end of the season that he didn't feel that his players and management team had been given the credit they deserved for winning the treble, and he was right. Scottish football is so derided – mainly by those in it – that it can be easy to underestimate just how difficult winning all three domestic prizes can be.

Managing to do it while rebuilding a squad and a culture at Ibrox makes the achievements of Dick Advocaat, his staff and his players all the more remarkable. The fact that rivals Celtic came alive after the break and almost matched Rangers stride for stride on the run-in to the end of the season may have made some of the public and media focus their attention elsewhere. But Rangers still out-paced them – and everybody else – to claim every prize.

They also did so while enduring a number of injuries to key players. Arthur Numan, for example, was a key member of Advocaat's strategy, and didn't kick a ball after the break. A pelvic injury to Barry Ferguson robbed Rangers of one of their most inspirational players, and a number of the striking options failed to fire, like Amato and Guivarc'h. But Rangers managed to iron out early season frailties at the back, and captain Lorenzo Amoruso emerged from the season a stronger, more confident figure. Advocaat had managed to make his new squad a team which had spirit and style in just ten months.

Icing On The Cake: There's nothing quite like a Scottish Cup win against Celtic – especially when it completes the treble.

Left: As usual, Rodney Wallace, leaving players in his wake.

Below left: New Boy Makes Good: The young Lee Feeney is tipped to be big at Ibrox.

Below right: Lorenzo Amoruso is given a talking-to during the Scottish Cup Final.

No one could grudge them either their prizes, or the Manager of the Year title which Advocaat won.

While some signings were less successful, others were inspired. Rod Wallace's total of 27 goals was a vitally important contribution. Giovanni van Bronckhorst blossomed into an essential part of midfield and Jorg Albertz almost re-invented himself, confirming to his manager what most of the fans already believed, that he can be an inspirational player on his day. And then there was the signing of Neil McCann. Used either on the wing or through the middle, he has thrived under Advocaat's tutelage and become the scorer of vital goals. He kept a cool head amongst the bedlam of the championship-clinching game at Parkhead to score two of the goals which took Rangers to victory.

Advocaat re-fashioned Rangers, but put them back to where the fans expect them to be – at the top. And even the presence of Advocaat seemed to boost the image of the club and Scottish football as a whole. He is a figure who is respected around the world, and it shouldn't be forgotten that he turned down a more lucrative offer to manage Real Madrid because he had given his word to David Murray that he was coming to Ibrox. The Dutchman has brought many new ideas to Scotland, but there is one we could have thought of ourselves – the standard of Scottish football and footballers isn't as bad as some claim.

Rising to the occasion: Colin Hendry is the man on the ball.

One fact is indisputable. Advocaat came, he saw, and his team conquered Scotland.

Rangers' Giovanni van Bronckhorst and Celtic's Henrik Larsson going for the ball. As happened so often last season, Rangers won.

Up for the Cup: Rangers captain Lorenzo Amoruso proudly lifts the Scottish Premier League trophy for the first time.

	P	W	D	L	F	A	Pts
RANGERS	36	23	8	5	78	31	77
Celtic	36	21	8	7	84	35	71
St Johnstone	36	15	12	9	39	38	57
Kilmarnock	36	14	14	8	47	29	56
Dundee	36	13	7	16	36	56	46
Hearts	36	11	9	16	44	50	42
Motherwell	36	10	11	15	35	54	41
Aberdeen	36	10	7	19	43	71	37
Dundee Utd	36	8	10	18	37	48	34
Dunfermline	36	4	16	16	28	59	28

PREVIOUS TREBLES

1948-49

In 1948-49 Rangers became the first team to win the glorious treble of the League Championship, Scottish Cup and League Cup. In the qualifying sections of the League Cup Rangers were drawn with Celtic, and 105,000 fans watched the Ibrox side beat their greatest rivals 2-1 to clinch a place in the quarter-finals. Rangers beat St. Mirren 1-0 and Dundee 4-1 on their way to a final against Raith Rovers.
A 2-0 victory saw them complete the first leg of the treble. Rangers were rampant in the Scottish Cup. They beat Elgin, Motherwell, Partick and then East Fife on their way to the Final, scoring 17 goals and conceding just one. In the final, Rangers met Clyde and won the Cup with a memorable 4-1 victory. The difficult bit was the Championship. Rangers and Dundee had been neck and neck all season, and on the final day the Ibrox side were at Albion Rovers while the Tayside team needed only a draw at Falkirk to win their first League title. Rangers stayed focused and a Willie Thornton hat-trick saw them win 4-1, but Dundee lost by the same score at Brockville and the title went to Ibrox. Rangers had made history by securing the first domestic clean sweep. It was the crowning season of Bill Struth's time as manager at Ibrox.

1963-64

Struth's successor, Scot Symon, delivered Rangers' second treble in the 1963-64 season. This time Rangers were rampant in the League – winning 25 out of their 34 matches and beating Celtic home and away. St Johnstone were the bogey side – recording the remarkable achievement of doing the double over Rangers. A 5-0 rout of Morton in the League Cup Final completed the first leg of the treble, and a 3-1 win over Dundee delivered the Scottish Cup and another clean sweep.

1975-76

Rangers had to wait 12 years for their next treble, but then two came along in three years, both with Jock Wallace as manager. In the inaugural year of the Premier Division, Rangers ran away with the Championship, winning 23 of their 36 League games, drawing eight and losing five.

They won both games at home against Celtic and drew the away games. A Derek Johnstone goal after 22 seconds delivered the title at Tannadice and Rangers' winning margin over Celtic was six points. Rangers had already won the League Cup by then, defeating Celtic 1-0 in the final and a Scottish Cup Final victory over Hearts completed the treble. Famously the Final kicked-off early and Rangers scored before three o'clock on their way to a 3-1 win.

1977-78

The next season was barren, but in 1977-78 Rangers won the treble again. This time their closest challengers were Aberdeen. Rangers again beat Celtic to clinch the League Cup, this time winning 2-1 in the spring sunshine. A 2-0 victory over Motherwell at Ibrox on the final day of the season secured the Championship and then they met Aberdeen in the Scottish Cup Final. Goals in each half from Alex MacDonald and Derek Johnstone won the final leg of the treble before the Dons got a late consolation.

1992-93

Walter Smith was the next Rangers manager to win the treble in the awesome season of 1992-93, when Rangers nearly got to the European Cup Final. Rangers lost only one of their first 23 League games and, of the other four defeats, three came after the Championship had been won. The flag stayed at Ibrox with a nine point advantage over Aberdeen, who they beat 2-1 to win it. The Dons had already been beaten 2-1 in the League Cup Final and a 2-0 victory over Airdrie secured the Scottish Cup. All three trophies were in the Ibrox trophy room for the fifth time and Smith's side had at one stage gone a remarkable 44 games without defeat in all competitions. That included 29 League games, four League Cup, three Scottish Cup and eight matches in the European Champions League.

Richard Gough proudly displays the Scottish Cup in 1993.

FIRST-TEAM FRIENDLIES

28 June 1998

vs. FC Molde – A: Lost 1-2 (Albertz 65)

Rangers: Niemi, Porrini, Petric, Amoruso, Stensaas, B Ferguson, Thern, Albertz, Johansson, Graham, Van Vossen

Substitutes: Wilson, Gattuso, Vidmar, Nicholson, Miller

30 June

vs. Asane – A: Won 3-1 (Miller 16, Vossen 28, Graham 79)

Rangers: Brown, Miller, Wilson, Amoruso, Vidmar, I. Ferguson, Gattuso, McInnes, Van Vossen, Miller, Albertz

Substitutes: Porrini, Petric, Stensaas, B Ferguson, Nicholson, Graham, Johansson, Thern

2 July

vs. Vossk – A: Won 6-0 (Gattuso 8, Johansson 53 86, Graham 71 80, Miller 76)

Rangers: Brown, Porrini, Amoruso, Petric, Vidmar, Thern, Gattuso, Johansson, Van Vossen, Albertz, I Ferguson

Substitutes: Miller, Wilson, Stensaas, Nicholson, Graham, B Ferguson, McInnes

14 July

vs. St Mirren – A: Won 2-0 (Albertz 2, Graham 90)

Rangers: Niemi, Porrini, Amoruso, Petric, Vidmar, Thern, B. Ferguson, I Ferguson, Amato, Johansson, Albertz

Substitutes: Stensaas, Gattuso, Graham, Miller, Nicholson

17 July

vs. Falkirk – A: Won 2-0 (Durie 35, Albertz 6 [pen])

Rangers: Charbonnier, Porrini, Moore, Petric, Stensaas, B. Ferguson, Gattuso, I Ferguson, Amato, Durie, Albertz

Substitutes: Vidmar, Thern, Miller, Graham

17 January 1999

vs. Atletico Mineiro – A: Draw 2-2 (Guivarc'h 36 43) [Rangers lost 4-5 on Penalties] Scorers: McCann, Johansson, Feeney, Hendry

Rangers: Klos, Vidmar, Hendry, Amoruso, Stensaas, Miller, Kanchelskis, Albertz, Wallace, Guivarc,h, McCann

Substitutes: Porrini, Niemi, van Bronckhorst, B. Ferguson, Johansson, Wilson, Feeney, Nicholson, Amato

2 March

vs. Middlesbrough – H: Draw 4-4 (Fowler 6, Guivarc'h 63, McLaren 73 [pen], Wallace 89

Rangers: Klos, Nicholson, Hendry, Wilson, McLaren, Wilkins*, Kanchelskis, Miller, Amato, Fowler*, van Bronckhorst

Substitutes: Gascoigne*, Guivarc,h, Wallace, Pearce*, Vidmar, McInnes, Niemi, Johansson

*Ray Wilkins, Robbie Fowler, Paul Gascoigne and Stuart Pearce were all guests of Rangers for the evening

24 March

vs. Raith Rovers – A: Lost 0-1

Rangers: Klos, Porrini, Amoruso, Vidmar, McInnes, Carson, Kanchelskis, van Bronckhorst, Miller, Amato, Albertz

Substitutes: Wallace, Riccio, Brown, J Gibson, Malcolm, McKnight

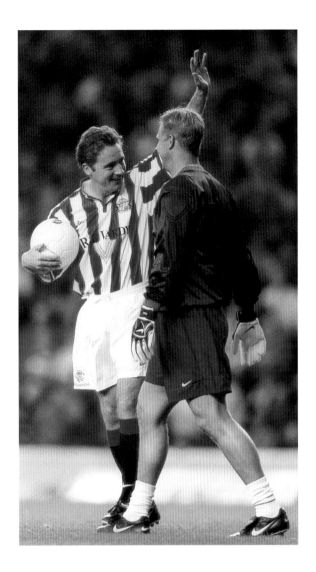

Below, left: Jonatan Johansson gets a taste of playing against foreign opposition in this first-team friendly against Sunderland.

Right: Familiar Faces: Former Rangers' favourites Ally McCoist, in an unfamiliar strip, greets Chris Woods during half-time at Rangers' 3-1 win over Sunderland.

FIRST-TEAM PRE-SEASON FRIENDLIES 1999-2000

July 10

vs. Livingston – A: Won 4-1 (Vidmar 3, Amato)

July 12

vs. St Mirren – A: Lost 1-2 (Albertz)

July 14

vs. Sogndal – A: Won 2-0 (Wallace, van Bronckhorst)

July 17

vs. Follese – A: Won 10-1 (Amato 3, Durie 2, Moore, Mols, van Bronckhorst, Wallace, Johansson)

July 19

vs. Rosenborg – A: Won 1-0 (Strand [og])

July 21

vs. Sunderland – H: Won 3-1 (B Ferguson, Bould [og], van Bronckhorst)

UNDER-18s 1998-99

The proud winners of the Glasgow Cup.

Winning the Glasgow Cup again was a highlight for the under-18 team, but just as with the under-21s it was the development of some of the players as individuals which bodes well for the future.

James and Billy Gibson, along with Robert Malcolm and Paul McKnight saw themselves elevated to the first team squad, even if it was for a late season friendly against Raith Rovers.

Maybe not the most important fixture of the season, but it shows that Dick Advocaat and Bert Van Lingen are looking to the younger players to stake a claim in Rangers' future.

29 August

vs. Dunfermline – H: Won 5-0 (McLean 3, Dobbie, Dewar)

Rangers: Snelders, Hughes, Morgan (Trialist), Malcolm, Dowie, B Gibson, McHale, Trialist, McLean (Kelly), Dobbie (Robb), Dewar

5 September

vs. Kilmarnock – A: Won 3-1 (Malcolm 3)

Rangers: Brown, Hughes, Trialist, Malcolm, Dowie, B Gibson, McHale, Russell (Morgan), McLean, Dobbie, Dewar

Bob Malcolm was a defensive regular in the Under-18 team.

12 September

vs. St Johnstone – A: Won 2-0 (B Gibson, McAdam)

Rangers: McGregor, Malcolm, Willoughby, Currie, McHale, Dewar, Dobbie (Trialist), B Gibson, Kelly (McAdam), Russell, Trialist

19 September

vs. Dundee United – H: Won 3-1 (Dobbie, B Gibson, Kelly)

Rangers: McGregor, Currie, Hughes, Malcolm, Willoughby, B Gibson, McHale, J Gibson, Kelly, Dobbie, Morrison (McAdam)

26 September

vs. Hibernian – A: Won 3-1 (J Gibson, Duffy, Malcolm)

Rangers: Niemi, Currie, Hughes, Malcolm, Willoughby, McHale, B Gibson, J Gibson, Dobbie (Carson), Duffy, Kelly

3 October

vs. Aberdeen – H: Lost 1-2 (Dobbie)

Rangers: Brown, Hughes, Trialist, Malcolm, Willoughby, B Gibson, McHale, J Gibson, Kelly (Middleton), Duffy, Dobbie (Carson)

17 October

vs. Dundee –H: Won 3–0 (Dobbie 2, Duffy)

Rangers: Brown, Currie, Hughes, Malcolm, Ross (Willoughby), B Gibson, McHale (McIntyre), J Gibson, Kelly (Duffy), Dobbie, Carson

24 October

vs. Hearts – A: Lost 0–2

Rangers: Brown, Currie, Hughes, Malcolm, Dowie, B Gibson, McHale (Willoughby), J Gibson, MacDonald, Dobbie (Duffy), Carson

Jim Gibson – midfield general – embraces the cup that means so much to him and his team mates.

14 November

vs. St Johnstone – H: Won 1-0 (Carson)

Rangers: McGregor, Currie, Morgan (Leven), Malcolm, Dowie, B Gibson, McHale, Hughes, MacDonald (Duffy), Dobbie (Kelly), Carson

21 November

vs. Dundee United – A: Drew 4-4 (MacDonald 3, B Gibson)

Rangers: McGregor, Hughes, Morgan, Malcolm, Currie, B Gibson, McHale, Morrison, Kelly (MacDonald), Dobbie (Duffy), Carson

Defender Ross Currie leaves a Celtic player in his wake in the game that bought yet another cup to Ibrox.

Stuart Kelly goes for goal with an athletic shot in Rangers' 3-0 victory over Dundee.

Paul McHale, a regular in the midfield, shows his dribbling skills in the season's final match against Celtic.

Steve Carson: Northern Ireland-born midfielder was never afraid to get stuck in to the action.

23 January

vs. Hearts – H: Won 3-1 (Dobbie, MacDonald, McAdam)

Rangers: Brown, Dobbie (Duffy), Hughes, Malcolm, Ross, Dowie, McHale, J Gibson, MacDonald, McAdam (Morrison), Carson

28 January

vs. Kilmarnock – H: Won 2-1 (Malcolm, McHale)

Line-up: McGregor, Dowie, Hughes, Malcolm, Ross, Dobbie (B Gibson), McHale, J Gibson, MacDonald, McAdam, Carson (Dewar)

12 March

vs. Hibernian – H: Won 2-0 (Dobbie, Dewar)

Rangers: Brown, Currie, Hughes, Dowie, Ross, B Gibson, Dewar (Trialist), J Gibson, Duffy, Dobbie (Kelly), Carson

1 April

vs. Celtic – A: Lost 1-2 (Malcolm)

Rangers: McGregor, Dowie, Hughes, Malcolm, Ross, B Gibson, McHale, J Gibson, MacDonald, Trialist (Dobbie), Carson

16 April

vs. Dunfermline – A: Drew 0-0

Rangers: McGregor, Dowie, Currie, Malcolm, Ross, B Gibson, McHale, J Gibson, MacDonald, Dewar (Hughes), Carson

1 May

vs. Dundee – A: Won 3-0 (Dobbie, Currie, J Gibson)

Rangers: Snelders, Dowie, Willoughby, Hughes, Ross, B Gibson, McHale (Duffy), J Gibson, Dobbie (MacDonald), Currie, Dewar

14 May

vs. Aberdeen – A: Lost 0-1

Rangers: Niemi, Willoughby, Currie (Duffy), Malcolm, Ross, Hughes, McHale, J Gibson, MacDonald, Dobbie (Kelly), Dewar (Robison)

28 May

vs. Celtic – H: Won 2-0 (MacDonald 2)

Rangers: Brown, Hughes, Malcolm, Dowie, Dewar, McHale, J Gibson, MacDonald, Dobbie (Kelly), Carson (Duffy), Currie

UNDER-21s 1998-99

The new emphasis on youth development from Dick Advocaat coincided with the SPL scrapping reserve team football and setting up an under-21 league. The commitment to younger players can be seen with the team being weakened when players like Barry Nicholson were promoted to the first team squad. There is now the real belief in the under-21s that if they perform they will get their first team break.

21 August

vs. Hearts – H: Lost 0-1

Rangers: Brown, Malcolm, Riccio, Wilson, Stone, Stensaas, Fitzgerald (McHale), McInnes, Negri, Graham, McKnight (J Gibson). Subs not used: B Gibson, Willoughby

27 August

vs. Kilmarnock – A: Drew 1-1 (Graham)

Rangers: Brown, Stone, Riccio, Wilson, Prodan, Nicholson, Fitzgerald, McInnes, Graham, McKnight (Malcolm), Boyack Subs (not used): McHale, B Gibson, Dewar

31 August

vs. Motherwell – A: Drew 3-3 (Boyack, Fitzgerald, Graham)

Rangers: Brown, Malcolm, Riccio, Prodan, Stone, B Gibson, Fitzgerald, Boyack, Graham, Rozental (McLean) (McHale), McKnight

16 September

vs. Dundee United – H: Lost 0-1

Rangers: Brown, Stone, Riccio, Wilson, Prodan, B Gibson, J Gibson (Willoughby), McInnes, Fitzgerald, Rozental, McHale Subs not used: Currie, McGregor, Kelly

21 September

vs. St Johnstone – A: Won 1-0 (Boyack)

Rangers: Niemi, Malcolm, Riccio, Wilson, Stone, Gattuso (J Gibson), Fitzgerald, Miller (B Gibson), Graham, Rozental, Boyack

29 September

vs. Aberdeen – H: Won 3-0 (Graham, Fitzgerald, McHale)

Rangers: Niemi, Malcolm, Riccio, Wilson, Stone, B Gibson, Miller, McHale, Graham, Rozental, Fitzgerald Subs (not used): Willoughby, Brown, Currie, Kelly

3 November

vs. Dunfermline – A: Won 5-0 (Stensaas, B Gibson, Fitzgerald 2, Boyack)

Rangers: Niemi (Brown), Malcolm, Riccio, Stone, Petric, B Gibson (Young), Stensaas, J Gibson (McHale), Fitzgerald, Graham, Boyack

12 November

vs. Hearts – A: Drew 2–2 (Fitzgerald, Nicholson)

Rangers: Brown, Young, Riccio, Stensaas, Stone, Nicholson, McHale (McDonald), Boyack, Fitzgerald, Durie (McKnight), Graham

25 November

vs. Motherwell – H: Lost 0-3

Rangers: Brown, Young, Riccio, Stensaas, Malcolm, Nicholson, B Gibson, Miller (McHale), Fitzgerald, McKnight, Boyack

1 December

vs. Dundee United – A: Drew 1-1 (Boyack)

Rangers: Snelders, Young (MacDonald), Riccio, Vidmar, Malcolm, Nicholson, McHale, J Gibson, McKnight, Boyack, Stensaas

14 December

vs. Aberdeen – A: Drew 1-1 (Amato)

Rangers: Snelders, Young (Malcolm), Riccio, Ross (B Gibson), Stone, Nicholson, Stensaas, Miller, Fitzgerald, Amato, McKnight

1 February

vs. Dunfermline – H: Won 3-1 (Feeney 2, Amato)

Rangers: Niemi, B Gibson (Dewar), Riccio, Ross, Stone (Currie), Feeney, Young, Thern (McHale), Fitzgerald, Amato, Johansson

26 February

vs. Kilmarnock – H: Lost 0-2

Rangers: Niemi (J Brown), B Gibson, Hughes, Riccio, Ross, Young, McHale, Nicholson, Fitzgerald, McKnight (Kelly), Dewar (Currie)

4 March

vs. Dundee United – H: Drew 1-1 (McKnight)

Rangers: Brown, B Gibson, Currie, Ross, Riccio, Young, McHale, J Gibson, Fitzgerald, McKnight, Carson (Dewar)

11 March

vs. St Johnstone – A: Won 4-2 (Johansson 2, Miller, Amato)

Rangers: Niemi, B Gibson, J Gibson (McHale), Ross, Malcolm, Nicholson, Fitzgerald, Miller, Johansson (McKnight), Amato, Young (Feeney)

16 March

vs. Aberdeen – H: Lost 0-1

Rangers: Niemi, B Gibson, Riccio, Ross, Malcolm, Feeney, J Gibson, Miller, McKnight, Fitzgerald, Carson (Hughes)

27 March

vs. Celtic – H: Won 2-0 (McKnight, McHale)

Rangers: Brown, B Gibson, Riccio, Ross, Malcolm, Gibson, Hughes, McInnes, McKnight, McHale, Carson

5 April

vs. Dundee – A: Won 1–0 (Guivarc'h)

Rangers: Niemi, Ross, Riccio (B Gibson), Wilson, Hendry (McHale), Nicholson, Feeney, McInnes, Guivarc'h, McKnight, Carson (Fitzgerald)

12 April

vs. Hearts – H: Won 2-0 (MacDonald, Fitzgerald)

Rangers: Niemi, Stone (Robison), Willoughby, Ross, Malcolm (Hughes), Gibson, McHale, MacDonald, Fitzgerald, Dobbie, Feeney (Kelly)

16 April

vs. Dundee – H: Won 3-2 (Feeney, Kelly, Nicholson)

Rangers: Brown, Robison, Currie, Stone, Willoughby, Feeney, Dobbie (Ross), Nicholson, Fitzgerald, MacDonald, Kelly

20 April

vs. Dunfermline – A: Won 2-1 (Fitzgerald, Ross)

Rangers: Brown, B Gibson, Currie, Wilson, Ross, Nicholson, McHale, Feeney, Fitzgerald, McKnight, Carson (MacDonald)

24 April

vs. Celtic – A: Lost 0-4

Rangers: Niemi, B Gibson, Currie, Stone, Malcolm, J Gibson, Feeney, McHale, Fitzgerald, Hughes, Carson (Kelly)

29 April

vs. Celtic – A: Lost 1-3 (B Gibson)

Rangers: Brown, B Gibson, Currie (Hughes), Ross, Stone, Riccio, McHale (Dewar), J Gibson, Fitzgerald (Kelly), McKnight (Dobbie), Feeney

4 May

vs. Motherwell – A: Won 1-0 (Nicholson)

Rangers: Snelders, B Gibson (Willoughby), Currie, Ross, Stone, J Gibson (MacDonald), McHale, Nicholson, Fitzgerald, Feeney, Hughes (Kelly)

18 May

vs. Kilmarnock – A: Lost 1-2 (I Ferguson)

Rangers: Brown, Robison (Hughes), Willoughby (Stone), McHale, Riccio, J Gibson, I Ferguson (MacDonald 65), Nicholson, Kelly, Fitzgerald, Feeney

20 May

vs. St Johnstone – H: Drew 1-1 (Fitzgerald)

Rangers: Niemi, Currie (Robison), Riccio, Malcolm, Stone (Willoughby), Feeney, Carson, Nicholson, Fitzgerald, McKnight (J Gibson), MacDonald

22 May

vs. Dundee – H: Won 3-0 (Dobbie, Malcolm, Feeney)

Rangers: Niemi, Dowie, Currie, Stone, Malcolm, Feeney, Dewar (Kelly), I Ferguson (J Gibson), Fitzgerald, Duffy (MacDonald), Duffy

1999-2000

THE SQUAD

Back row: Feeney, Johansson, Vidmar, Niemi, Klos, Brown, Albertz, Wilson, Moore, Hendry

Middle row: Van Lingen, Nicholson, B Ferguson, Amato, Porrini, Durie, I Ferguson, Kanchelskis, Negri, Adamczuk

Front row: Wallace, McCann, van Bronckhorst, Amoruso, Advocaat, Numan, Mols, Reyna

Foreground: Scottish Cup, Premier League Trophy, League Cup

Dariusz ADAMCZUK

Squad number

17

Position

midfielder

Born

21 October 1969

Warsaw

Poland

Rangers beat Celtic to the signature of Adamczuk after he left Dundee under freedom of contract in the summer.

The Polish international is a versatile player who can play either in midfield or at the back. He was the midfield anchor during his five years at Dens Park, but it seems Advocaat sees him more as a wing-back.

A good ball winner, Adamczuk also has good vision and passes the ball well. At first it was thought he would just be a squad player, but Adamczuk has made it clear he will fight all the way to establish himself as a first team regular.

Jorg ALBERTZ

Squad number

11

Position

Midfielder

Born

29 January 1971

Moenchengladbach

Germany

Since joining Rangers for £4 million from Hamburg, Jorg Albertz has become a firm favourite with the Ibrox supporters. He never missed a game during his three seasons with the German club, scoring 22 goals in 99 League appearances. He earned the nickname 'the Hammer' for his spectacular goals and his reputation has grown with a number of crucial goals since joining the Ibrox side in the summer of 1996. His shooting was measured at 80mph in a speed test and the German international scored his first hat-trick for Rangers in the club's 6-1 League victory over Dundee in February 1999.

Gabriel AMATO

Squad number
15
Position
Striker
Born
22 October 1970
Mar Del Plata
Argentina

Gabriel Amato signed for Rangers from Spanish side Real Mallorca in the summer of 1998 for £4.2 million. Amato played for a number of clubs in his home country, including top club side River Plate, before moving to Europe. He established himself as a premium quality striker in Spain's Primera Liga and debuted for Rangers in the UEFA Cup against Shelbourne where he sensationally scored two goals to take the Ibrox side to a 5-3 victory. He played in the return leg as a substitute and got his first start in the Scottish Premier League in the 2-1 win over Motherwell in August 1998.

Lorenzo AMORUSO

Squad number
4
Position
Defender
Born
28 June 1971
Palese
Italy

Club captain Lorenzo Amoruso signed for Rangers during the 1997-98 season for £4 million. Before coming to Ibrox he played for a number of teams in Italy including Bari and Fiorentina, his club before joining Rangers. He debuted for Rangers against Celtic at Parkhead and went on to play four times for the club before an injury to his Achilles tendon kept him out of the game for ten months. Despite this, Dick Advocaat named him club captain at the beginning of the 1998-99 season and he went on to lift his first trophy when Rangers won against St Johnstone in the League Cup Final on November 29.

Giovanni VAN BRONCKHORST

Squad number

8

Position

Midfielder

Born

5 February 1975

Rotterdam

Holland

Midfielder Giovanni van Bronckhorst signed for Rangers in the summer of 1998 for £5.25 from Dutch club Feyenoord. The second of Advocaat's signings from the Dutch international team which made it to the semi-finals of the World Cup, van Bronckhorst was rated as one of Feyenoord's top players and the Rangers manager faced stiff opposition to capture the player. He made his debut for the Ibrox side at left-back, scoring in the 5-3 victory over Shelbourne in the UEFA Cup.

Lionel CHARBONNIER

Squad number

22

Position

Goalkeeper

Born

25 October 1966

Poitiers

France

Goalkeeper Lionel Charbonnier was signed from Auxerre for £1.2 million in the summer of 1998. Ever since Auxerre beat Rangers 2-1 in the 1996-97 Champions League, he had wanted to join the club, and his excellent performances quickly made him a favourite with the Ibrox support when he did sign. He made his debut for Rangers in the 2-1 League victory over Motherwell in August 1998, notching up 19 consecutive appearances for the team in goal. However, a knee injury sustained during the UEFA Cup tie against Bayer Leverkusen at Ibrox in November sidelined him for the rest of the season.

Gordon DURIE

Squad number

24

Position

Striker

Born

6 December 1965

Paisley

Scotland

Rangers' most experienced player, Durie has played over 400 games in League football during his career. He started out at East Fife when he was 16, before moving to Hibernian for two seasons. He then spent nine years south of the border with Chelsea and Tottenham before signing for Rangers in 1993-94 for £1.2 million. He was also a member of the 1998 Scottish World Cup Squad, playing in all three of the national side's games during the tournament. He has had many notable moments since joining Rangers, including becoming the first Ibrox player to score a hat-trick in a Scottish Cup Final when Rangers beat Hearts 5-1 in 1996. Unfortunately his 1998-99 season was cut short after an ankle operation in Feburary.

Barry FERGUSON

Squad number

6

Position

Midfielder

Born

2 February 1978

Glasgow

Scotland

Barry Ferguson joined Rangers as a schoolboy and has gone on to earn a reputation as one of Scotland's fastest-rising young football stars. He made his debut for the first team against Hearts on the last day of the 1996-97 season, where he was voted Man of the Match. He went onto make seven League appearances the following season and, since the arrival of Advocaat, he has had a regular starring role in central midfield, scoring his first League goal during the club's 2-1 victory over Dunfermline in September 1998. He has also seen international success, earning his first cap for Scotland in the European Championship qualifier against Lithuania.

Ian FERGUSON

Squad number
26
Position
Midfielder
Born
15 March 1967
Glasgow
Scotland

Ian Ferguson remains the only player still at Ibrox who was a member of all the nine-in-a-row Championship-winning teams. He joined Rangers during the 1987-88 season, having previously enjoyed success with Clyde and St Mirren. In the 1987 Scottish Cup Final he scored the winning goal for the Paisley team against Dundee. Since joining Rangers, Ferguson has played in 204 League games, scoring 21 goals from midfield. Unfortunately he suffered an ankle injury during a game with Hearts in August and missed the rest of the season.

Colin HENDRY

Squad number
16
Position
Defender
Born
7 December 1965
Keith
Scotland

Scotland's World Cup captain Colin Hendry returned to Scotland after 11 years in England when he signed for Rangers in August for £4 million. He had built up a reputation as a one of the finest central defenders in the FA Carling Premiership, a reputation cemented when he led Blackburn Rovers to League victory in 1994-95. Despite the years he spent south of the border, Hendry's football career started in his home town of Keith where he played in the Highland League. He later moved to Dundee as a centre-forward before transferring to Blackburn in 1987.

Jonatan JOHANSSON

Squad number

20

Position

Striker

Born

16 August 1975

Stockholm

Sweden

Finland International Jonatan Johansson joined Rangers for £500,000 from FC Flora in Estonia in August 1997 following a two-week trial. In his first season he made six League appearances for the club, mainly as a substitute. The 1998-99 season saw him establish a regular place in the first team where he has shown an ability to score crucial goals. On hearing that an offer for him had been received from Derby County just before Christmas 1998, he decided he wanted to remain at Ibrox.

Andrei KANCHELSKIS

Squad number

7

Position

Midfielder

Born

23 January 1969

Kirovgrad

Ukraine

Andrei Kanchelskis was a record signing when he joined the Ibrox Club for £5.5 million from Italian Serie A side Fiorentina in July 1998. The Ukrain who plays for the Russian national side made his debut for the club in the 2-1 victory over Shelbourne in the UEFA cup and has since become a first team regular. Kanchelskis' football career began at 15 when he was sent to a school for gifted footballers and spent time with Dynamo Kiev before moving Shakhtyor Donetsk. In March 1991 he joined Manchester United and finished the 1994-95 season as the club's top scorer. However following a dispute he was transferred to Everton and then to Fiorentina in 1997.

Stefan KLOS

Squad number

1

Position

Goalkeeper

Born

16 July 1971

Dortmund

Germany

Stefan Klos signed for Rangers for £700,000 from Borussia Dortmund on Christmas Eve 1998, replacing the injured Charbonnier in the first team. Rangers had been interested in the player for over a year before the signing was made, but a contract dispute with Dortmund prevented him from making the move. Klos debuted for Rangers on Boxing Day in the 1-0 win over St Johnstone in the Premier League. Klos brought experience of European competition to Rangers – including his appearance in the Dortmund team which won the European Cup in May 1997.

Neil McCANN

Squad number

18

Position

Striker

Born

11 July 1974

Greenock

Scotland

Scottish international Neil McCann joined Rangers from Hearts in December 1998 for £1.6 million. He began his career with Dundee, making his first League appearance for the Dens Park side in the 1992-93 season. In July 1996 he signed for Hearts where he played in 73 League games scoring 18 goals. He debuted for Rangers in the 3-2 victory at Tynecastle in December and scored his first goal for the Ibrox side in the 6-0 rout of Hamilton in the Fourth Round of the Tennents Scottish Cup at Firhill in February 1999.

Michael MOLS

Squad number

9

Position

Striker

Born

17 December 1970

Amsterdam

Holland

Mols made a spectacular start to his Rangers career with a double against FC Haka in a Champions League qualifier. The Dutchman has pace and can turn on the proverbial sixpence. The £4 million deal which brought him from FC Utrecht was signed last season, but he didn't arrive at Ibrox until the summer. That gave the Utrecht fans the time to get up a petition in a last-ditch attempt to persuade him to stay at the club.

A prolific goalscorer with 17 goals in 28 appearances last season, Dick Advocaat expects the 28 year old to improve under his tutelage.

Craig MOORE

Squad number

3

Position

Defender

Born

12 December 1975

Sydney

Australia

Signed by Walter Smith, it wasn't until Advocaat came to Ibrox that Craig Moore started to show his true form. Looking a lot more comfortable in the centre of defence than at full-back, the Australian left the club in October in a £3 million move to Crystal Palace in the hope of more regular first team football.

With the London club in financial difficulties he returned to Rangers at the end of March and is now prepared to fight for his place in Advocaat's first team.

Marco NEGRI

Squad number

21

Position

Striker

Born

27 October 1970

Milan

Italy

The return of Marco Negri to the Rangers squad is like the return of the prodigal son. The Italian signed on at Ibrox in June 1997 in a £4 million move from Perugia. He made an immediate impact, scoring all five goals in a demolition of Dundee United, and scored a phenomenal 32 goals in 29 games. But Negri then fell out with then manager Walter Smith.

He was farmed out to Italy on loan last season, but now seems to have patched things up with the Rangers management. If he can knuckle down and reproduce the form which he showed at the start of his career then all could be forgiven. A tremendous goal poacher when he is in the mood.

Barry NICHOLSON

Squad number

23

Position

Defender

Born

24 August 1978

Dumfries

Scotland

Midfielder Barry Nicholson progressed through the junior ranks at Ibrox, making his senior debut for the team in the 4-0 win against Dundee in January 1999. He has praised the youth policy which has provided him with a confident start to his career as one of the best in the country.

Antti NIEMI

Squad number

13

Position

Goalkeeper

Born

31 May 1972

Oulu

Finland

Bought from FC Copenhagen for £700,000 at the start of the 1997-98 season, the Finland international keeper initially joined Rangers at as an understudy for Andy Goram. However, he went on to make five League appearances later in the season and was in goal for the first four games of 1998-99. Despite over 20 caps for Finland, Niemi later found himself playing second fiddle to Charbonnier and then Klos, and announced in February 1999 that he was considering his future at the club.

Arthur NUMAN

Squad number

5

Position

Defender

Born

14 December 1969

Heemskerk

Holland

Arthur Numan signed for Rangers for £4.5 million just two weeks after playing for Holland in the 1998 World Cup. He has a long history with manager Advocaat, having already played for him at Haarlem and PSV Eindhoven. Regarded as one of the finest left-backs in Europe, Numan made his debut for Rangers when the team beat Shelbourne 2-1 in the UEFA cup. However, an ankle injury he sustained when playing against Kilmarnock just before Christmas led to Numan missing the rest of the season.

Sergio PORRINI

Squad number

2

Position

Defender

Born

11 November 1968

Milan

Italy

Sergio Porrini has been a regular in the Rangers first team since signing for the club from Juventus in the summer of 1997. The £3 million player had previously played in two European Cup Finals for Juve, winning the competition in 1997 when his team beat Ajax in a penalty shoot-out. He played his first match for Rangers in the qualifying round of the Champions League in 1996-97 when the Ibrox side beat GI Gotu 6-1. He scored his first goal for Rangers against Motherwell in September 1997 and has continued to display his exceptional skills ever since.

Daniel PRODAN

Squad number

25

Position

Defender

Born

23 March 1972

Satu Mare

Romania

Despite signing for Rangers in July 1998 for £2.2 million from Atletico Madrid, Daniel Prodan has been unable to take his place in the Rangers side due to a knee injury which is yet to clear up. However, the defender has a reputation across Europe as a first-class defender, notching up over 40 caps for the Romanian national team.

Claudio REYNA

Squad number

12

Position

Midfielder

Born

20 July 1973

New Jersey

America

The US international Claudio Reyna joined Rangers late in the 1998-99 season after impressing Dick Advocaat with his international and club record. As well as making 65 appearances for his country he was the first American to lead a European side when he captained his previous club Wolfsburg.

Tony VIDMAR

Squad number

14

Position

Defender

Born

4 July 1970

Adelaide

Australia

Australian 'Socceroo' International Tony Vidmar signed for Rangers from the Dutch side NAC Breda, a club he made 62 appearances for in two seasons, scoring four goals. A talented full-back, he played in 12 League games during his first season with the Ibrox club, scoring his first goal during Rangers' 6-0 win over Hamilton in the Fourth Round of the Scottish League Cup in 1999.

Rod WALLACE

Squad number
10
Position
Striker
Born
2 October 1969
Lewisham
London

Rod Wallace joined the Ibrox side on a free transfer from Leeds United in the summer of 1998. He scored his first goal for Rangers during his League debut against Heart on the opening day of the 1998-99 season. He soon became one of the team's most influential players, scoring in his first three games and against PAOK Salonika and Motherwell. Wallace began his career as a 16-year-old trainee at Southampton, before moving to Leeds for £1.6 million in 1991. The England B international's two brothers have also succeeded in the game, with Danny, his elder brother, playing for Manchester United and twin Ray also played for Leeds.

Scott WILSON

Squad number
19
Position
Defender
Born
19 March 1977
Edinburgh
Scotland

A product of the club's youth policy, Scott Wilson, has already had a taste of European football after lining up beside Richard Gough when Rangers played Ajax in the European Champions League – at the age of only 19. He also appeared for the Ibrox side when they beat Bayer Leverkusen 2-1 in the 1998-99 UEFA Cup. A member of the Scotland Under-21 squad, Wilson is dedicated to eventually achieving a regular place in Rangers' first team.

Mark BROWN

Squad number
32
Position
Goalkeeper
Born
28 February 1981
Motherwell

Lee FEENEY

Squad number
31
Position
Midfielder
Born
21 March 1978
Belfast
Northern Ireland

Jim GIBSON

Squad number
41
Position
Midfielder
Born
19 February 1980
Bellshill

Steven CARSON

Squad number
44
Position
Midfielder
Born
6 October 1980
Ballymoney

Darran FITZGERALD

Squad number
42
Position
Striker
Born
13 October 1978
Belfast
Northern Ireland

Derek McINNES

Squad number
27
Position
Midfielder
Born
5 July
Paisley

Iain CHALMERS

Squad number
43
Position
Defender
Born
26 August 1981
Glasgow

Billy GIBSON

Squad number
40
Position
Defender
Born
1 August 1981
Bellshill

Paul McKNIGHT

Squad number
28
Position
Striker
Born
8 February 1977
Belfast
Northern Ireland

Peter MACDONALD

Squad number

38

Position

Striker

Born

17 November 1981

Glasgow

Charlie MILLER

Squad number

29

Position

Midfielder

Born

18 March 1976

Glasgow

Michael STONE

Squad number

35

Position

Defender

Born

15 January 1979

Stirling

Steven MACADAM

Squad number

39

Position

Striker

Born

3 May 1981

Glasgow

Maurice ROSS

Squad number

34

Position

Defender

Born

3 February 1981

Dundee

Kirk WILLOUGHBY

Squad number

36

Position

Defender

Born

28 January 1981

Cambridge

Robert MALCOLM

Squad number

33

Position

Defender

Born

12 November 1980

Glasgow

Staale STENSAAS

Squad number

30

Position

Defender

Born

7 July 1971

Trondheim

Norway

David YOUNG

Squad number

37

Position

Midfielder

Born

1 March 1979

Glasgow

1999-2000

SPL OPPONENTS

ABERDEEN

Another disappointing season last term saw Aberdeen finish eighth in the table and get rid of yet another manager. The players have been accused of under-performing, but you can't say they do that when they play Rangers.

Even though the Dons took only one point off Rangers last season, every encounter was a close one and there is no reason to think it will be any different this season.

They have decided to bring experience to the manager's seat, with Dane Ebbe Skovdahl leaving Brondby for Pittodrie. He turned to Ibrox for his assistant, appointing Tommy Moller-Nielsen as his number two, the latter giving up his role as Dick Advocaat's first team coach.

Skovdahl struggled to bring in new faces before the season started, but is bound to strengthen the squad as the season goes on. He will be hoping that existing players start performing to their potential as Eoin Jess did last season.

Manager
Ebbe Skovdahl
Ground/capacity
Pittodrie/21,634
Nickname
The Dons
Position 1998-99
Eighth

Giovanni van Bronckhorst races past one of the Dons during November's League game at Ibrox. The Gers won 2-1.

Last Season vs. Rangers (League)		**Pittodrie**	1-1	4-2
(Rangers' score shown first)		**Ibrox**	2-1	3-1

CELTIC

Manager
Kenny Dalglish
Ground/capacity
Celtic Park/60,294
Nickname
The Bhoys, The Hoops
Position 1998-99
Runners-up

With the arrival of Kenny Dalglish as Director of Football and John Barnes as Head Coach, this year's challenge from Parkhead is likely to be even stronger than in previous seasons.

Dalglish immediately opened the Parkhead cheque book when he got there on 1 July 1999, and his £5 million capture, Eyal Berkovic from West Ham, is sure to make an impact on the Premier League.

Other signings like Bulgarian Stillian Petrov, Frenchman Olivier Tebily and Bobby Petta from Ipswich Town will further strengthen the Parkhead side.

Barnes is determined to play an attacking-passing game, and is trying to model his side on the 4-2-2-2 formation which teams like Brazil use, with overlapping full-backs as key players.

Celtic will be better prepared than they were last season and can surely be expected to challenge for honours right from the start.

Giovanni van Bronckhorst finds his way through blocked by a Celtic player. Skipper Amoruso thinks it's a foul.

Last Season vs. Rangers (League)			
(Rangers' score shown first)	Celtic Park	1-5	3-0
	Ibrox	0-0	2-2

DUNDEE

Manager
Jocky Scott
Ground/capacity
Dens Park/13,565
Nickname
The Dees, The Dark Blues
Position 1998-99
Fifth

Jorg Albertz shows that he's got what it takes to play football the hard way – even against Lee Maddison.

Jocky Scott's side were tipped to go down last season, but they surprised everybody, and a number of spirited performances saw them finish fifth in the Premier League.

When they held Rangers to a draw at Tannadice last season, Dick Advocaat said on the form they showed that day they could match anybody. They are not a team of stars, but have a squad who all work for each other.

Scott will be disappointed to have lost Adamczuk and former Rangers winger Iain Anderson through freedom of contract in the summer, but goalkeeper Rob Douglas's decision to stay at Dens Park will ensure they have one of the best keepers in the League. Another Ibrox old boy, Steven Boyack, seems to be relishing his move to Tayside. The Dees are never easy to beat, and visiting the rebuilt Dens Park isn't something anyone will look forward to.

Last Season vs. Rangers (League)			
(Rangers' score shown first)	Dens Park	4-0	1-1
	Ibrox	1-0	6-1

DUNDEE UNITED

Manager
Paul Sturrock
Ground/capacity
Tannadice Park/14,208
Nickname
The Terrors
Position 1998-99
Ninth

Two wins, one draw and a loss are what the Gers took from the Terrors.

United had another brush with relegation last season, finishing in ninth place, as manager Paul Sturrock continues with his quest to rebuild the Tannadice side and recapture their former glory.

Sturrock has said he won't be able to do that overnight, but however long it takes him, United are still capable of pulling off some remarkable results. No one at Ibrox needs to be told that, after the Terrors inflicted Rangers' first home defeat on Dick Advocaat and the team in the run-in to last season's title.

The man who scored the winner that day, Kjell Olfosson, has left the club, but with Billy Dodds up front United will always be dangerous on the break. Former Celt David Hannah will provide dig in midfield, while Sturrock will be looking to youngsters like Craig Easton and Steven Thompson to establish themselves in the first team.

Last Season vs. Rangers (League)			
(Rangers' score shown first)	Tannadice Park	0-0	2-1
	Ibrox	2-1	0-1

HEART OF MIDLOTHIAN

Jim Jefferies' side had a disappointing season last term, considering their Scottish Cup win and League challenge in 1998. Hampered by injuries, and after the loss of Neil McCann to Ibrox, Jefferies found it difficult to put out a settled side, and a number of new signings like Gary McSwegan and Vincent Guerin struggled to settle in to the team.

But the chances are that this term they will show their true potential and challenge once again. In the run-in last term, Jefferies added Darren Jackson from Celtic to his squad, as well as giant centre-half Kevin James from Falkirk, and both made an early impact. Despite their poor showing – sixth place in the League – Hearts were still a tough prospect at Tynecastle last season, but the good away form which had been a vital part of their title push the year before eluded them. Jefferies now has more depth to his squad and if his players can avoid the injury problems of last term then they are likely to have part to play in where this season's title will end up.

Manager
Jim Jeffries
Ground/capacity
Tynecastle/18,300
Nickname
The Jam Tarts, The Jambos
Position 1998-99
Sixth

Rod Wallace smashes in a shot, but it is parried to one side by the near-legendary keeper Jim Leighton.

Last Season vs. Rangers (League)		Tynecastle	1-2	3-2
(Rangers' score shown first)		Ibrox	3-0	0-0

HIBERNIAN

Manager
Alex McLeish
Ground/capacity
Easter Road/16,039
Nickname
The Hi-Bees
Position 1998-99
First Division Champions

After running away with the First Division last season, Hibs are back in the Premier League after a one year absence. Apart from winning promotion, manager Alex McLeish has built a strong squad with plenty of experience and quality in it. Franck Sauzee, who played in the Marseille side which took on Rangers in the Champions League in 1992, is now at Easter Road, in an almost entirely re-cast side from the one which was last in the top flight.

Up front, former Aberdeen striker Mixu Paatelainen is likely to partner former Fulham star Dirk Lehmann, but the man who pulls the strings in the side is Trinidad and Tobago international Russell Latapy. The slightly-built West Indian has a delightful touch and is deceptively strong.

McLeish has set his sights on more than Hibs just surviving now that they are back in the SPL, and he has assembled the kind of squad which could do well in the top ten.

Ally McCoist was overjoyed to score when Rangers met Hibs in the 1997-98 season.

Last Four vs. Rangers (1997-98 season) (Rangers' score shown first)		
Easter Road	4-3	2-1
Ibrox	1-0	3-0

KILMARNOCK

Robbed of a third place finish by St Johnstone on the last day of the season, Kilmarnock are still the likeliest team outside the Old Firm to challenge for the title. With former Rangers legends Ally McCoist and Ian Durrant in their side they certainly have enough experience of winning at the top.

In another former Ibrox stalwart Bobby Williamson, Killie have one of the most astute managers in the division and since he took over at Rugby Park they have won the Scottish Cup, in 1997, and have never been out of Europe.

Williamson's side is balanced throughout. He has a well-organised rearguard, and backs it up effectively with Celtic keeper Gordon Marshall, whose move to Ayrshire has revived his career.

Kilmarnock don't give away goals easily, have a blend of creativity and hard graft in midfield, and with Paul Wright, Jerome Vareille and McCoist up front, Williamson has plenty of options in attack. They certainly should be there or thereabouts again this term.

Manager
Bobby Williamson
Ground/capacity
Rugby Park/18,128
Nickname
The Killies
Position 1998-99
Fourth

Rod Wallace was back on scoring form right from the beginning of the 1999-2000 season.

Last Season vs. Rangers (League)		Rugby Park	3-1	5-0
(Rangers' score shown first)		Ibrox	1-0	1-1

MOTHERWELL

Manager
Billy Davies
Ground/capacity
Fir Park/13,742
Nickname
The Well
Position 1998-99
Seventh

Neil McCann shrugs off a stern challenge. Rangers beat Motherwell on three out of four occasions last year.

The Well are yet another Scottish Premier League side whose stars cut their teeth or made their names at Ibrox. The Fir Park side is managed by Billy Davies, captained by Andy Goram and kept ticking by John Spencer, all of whom need no introduction to Rangers fans.

Davies took over after the new regime of chairman John Boyle and player-Chief Executive Pat Nevin were installed and felt the highs and lows of management within a fortnight. In his first game he lost 5-0 to St Johnstone, but after bringing Spencer to Fir Park, the Lanarkshire side enjoyed a spirited 1-0 victory over Rangers.

Although not expected to challenge at the top, Motherwell are still a difficult prospect on their day.

Last Season vs. Rangers (League)	Fir Park	0-1	5-1
(Rangers' score shown first)	Ibrox	2-1	2-1

ST JOHNSTONE

Manager
Sandy Clark
Ground/capacity
McDiarmid Park/10,673
Nickname
The Saints
Position 1998-99
Third

The Saints celebrate European qualification on the last day of the 1998-99 season.

When former Rangers striker Sandy Clark took over at McDiarmid Park last season, the St Johnstone Chairman Geoff Brown predicted he would do better than his predecessor Paul Sturrock. In his first season he did: Saints enjoyed their highest finish ever in the Premier League with third place, and got to the League Cup Final and Scottish Cup semi-final – before being beaten by Rangers.

Sandy Clark's compact side all work for each other and are especially dangerous at home, where they beat Rangers once and Celtic twice last season. In Alan Main they have a great last line of defence – even if he did let in seven against the light blues – and in George O'Boyle they have one of the best poaching strikers in the League.

The Saints will find it difficult to better last season's efforts, but should still challenge at the top. Once again they might not look like winning the Championship, but they could have a great deal of influence over who does.

Last Season vs. Rangers (League)	McDiarmid Park	7-0	1-3
(Rangers' score shown first)	Ibrox	4-0	1-0

EUROPE

ALL TIME RESULTS

Rangers vs. Bayern Munich

1989-90
European Cup
Rangers 1-3 Bayern Munich
Bayern Munich 0-0 Rangers

1971-72
European Cup-Winners' Cup
Bayern Munich 1-1 Rangers
Rangers 2-0 Bayern Munich

1970-71
Fairs Cup
Bayern Munich 1-0 Rangers
Rangers 1-1 Bayern Munich

1966-67
European Cup-Winners' Cup
Bayern Munich 1-0 Rangers

Rangers vs. PSV Eindhoven

1978-79
European Cup
Rangers 0-0 PSV Eindhoven
PSV Eindhoven 2-3 Rangers

Rangers vs. Valencia

1979-80
European Cup-Winners' Cup
Valencia 1-1 Rangers
Rangers 1-3 Valencia

By beating Parma in August 1999, Rangers reached the last 32 in the UEFA Champions League – the first group stage. In this stage each team goes into one of eight groups of four teams, playing each team home and away for a total of six matches, played on Tuesday and Wednesday evenings. At the end of the first group stage, the top two teams in each group then go on to the second group stage. At that stage, the 16 remaining teams go into four groups of four, again playing home and away for a total of six matches.

The third-placed teams at the end of the first stage go into the third round of the UEFA Cup, while the teams finishing bottom in each group are out of Europe. At the end of the second group stage, the top two teams in each group qualify for the quarter-finals and the competition reverts to a knockout format, playing over two legs, home and away. The winners go on to the semi-finals which are played on the same basis. The final is a single match, with extra time and penalties, if necessary.

Group F

Just like in the last round of their Champions League qualifiers, Rangers got a tough, but very exciting draw and will be playing Germany's Bayern Munich, PSV Eindhoven from Holland and Valencia from Spain.

Last year's runners-up Bayern Munich looked to have their name on the trophy until Manchester United scored twice in the last minutes to win the European Cup. But Bayern

Another Bundesliga victory. Bayern will be hoping to avenge the 1999 Champions League Final.

Squad List   BAYERN MUNICH   Coach: Ottmar Hitzfeld

1 Oliver Kahn	8 Thomas Strunz	16 Jens Jeremies	22 Bernd Dreher
2 Markus Babbel	9 Giovane De Souza Elber	17 Thorsten Fink	23 Frank Wiblishauser
3 Bixente Lizarazu	10 Lothar Matthäus	18 Michael Tarnat	25 Thomas Linke
4 Osei Kuffour	11 Stefan Effenberg	19 Carsten Jancker	
5 Thomas Helmer	12 Sven Scheuer	20 Hasan Salihamidzic	
7 Mehmet Scholl	14 Mario Basler	21 Alexander Zickler	

Squad List   VALENCIA   Coach: Hector Cuper

1 José Cañizares	8 Francisco Farinos	15 Amedeo Carboni	23 David Albelda
2 Francisco Navarro	9 Oscar Garcia	16 Alain Roche	24 Daniel Fagiani
3 Joachim Björklund	10 Miguel Angulo	17 Juan Sanchez	25 Miguel Scoria
4 Francisco Camarasa	11 Adrian Ilie	18 Gabriel Popescu	26 Andres Palop
5 Miroslav Djukic	12 Cristian Gonzales	20 Jocelyn Angloma	28 Carlos Perez
6 Gaizka Mendieta	13 Jorge Bartual	21 Luis Milla	29 Jonathan Lopez
7 Claudio Lopez	14 Gerard Lopez	22 Denis Serban	30 Manuel Cabezas

are no strangers to Rangers; the two clubs seem to be destined to meet in Europe and have had several clashes over the years. The most notable matches were when the two met in the European Cup-Winners' Cup Final in 1967 when Bayern won 1-0, and when Rangers got revenge in the same competition in 1972 on the way to winning the tournament.

PSV Eindhoven are also no strangers to the Rangers – or certainly not manager Dick Advocaat as that was the club he left to come to Ibrox. The two sides have only met once in Europe, in the European Cup in 1978-79, when a Bobby Russell goal inflicted on PSV their first ever home defeat in Europe.

The following year Rangers had their only meeting against the third side in the group, Valencia. After a draw in Spain when Peter McCloy saved a penalty, Rangers lost the second leg at Ibrox, with Argentinian star Mario Kempes running riot.

Liverpool knocked Valencia out of the 1998-99 UEFA Cup.

PSV Eindhoven are back on the biggest European stage after a couple of years absence.

Squad List   PSV EINDHOVEN   Coach: Eric Gerets

1 Ivica Kralj	8 Ruud van Nistelrooij	17 Björn van der Doelen	24 Ovidiu Stinga
2 André Ooijer	9 Arnold Bruggink	18 Eric Addo	25 Stan Valckx
3 Jürgen Dirkx	10 Luc Nilis	19 Dennis Rommedahl	28 Tomasz Iwan
4 Ernest Faber	11 Joonas Kolkka	20 Patrick Lodewijiks	29 Georgi Gakhokidze
5 Jan Heintze	14 Johann Vogel	21 Iouri Nikiforov	30 Andrius Skerla
6 Mark van Bommel	15 Robert Fuchs	22 Wilfred Bouma	33 Robbie Wielaert
7 Dmitri Khokhlov	16 Chris van der Weerden	23 Ronald Waterreus	35 Abel Costa

Rangers' eclipse of Parma set alarm bells ringing throughout Europe, but if Dick Advocaat's team is to achieve the ultimate prize they must overcome the very best. Manchester United deserve that label at the moment, not only for lifting the European Cup last season, but for the manner in which they won it. Sir Alex Ferguson's team played with a combination of pride, passion and panache and defeated some of the continent's top clubs en route to victory. Barcelona, Inter Milan and Bayern Munich were among those who fell to the Old Trafford side and United's comparitively straightforward draw this year – they face Marseille, Croatia Zagreb and Sturm Graz – means they will be installed as favourites to retain the trophy.

Paolo Maldini: Captains one of Italy's most successful clubs, AC Milan.

Dwight Yorke scoring for Manchester United against Inter Milan in 1999. United won 2-0.

They will, of course, face stern opposition in the later stages of the competition. Most probably from Italian sides, who are always involved at the business end of European tournaments. Lazio, for instance, have spent tens of millions on making their biggest ever push for Champions League success. One look at their forward line is enough to induce palpations in defences throughout the length and breadth of the continent. Marcelo Salas, the Chilean World Cup striker, and Roberto Mancini will feed off the supply provided by

KEY PLAYERS

AC Milan

Andriy Shevchenko: In a star-studded line-up, the young Ukranian shines brightest. Every top club in Europe chased the 20-year-old's signature after his Champions League performances for Dynamo Kiev last year but Milan won the race and the striker will be their main threat up front in this campaign. Electrifying pace and deadly finishing, he's got the lot.

Manchester United

David Beckham: The best crosser of the ball in Europe, says his manager, and few would disagree. 'Becks' supplies endless ammunition for the likes of Dwight Yorke and Andy Cole, and does so with a swagger that excites United fans and infuriates opposition supporters. He is also a brilliant exponent of the art of taking free kicks.

S.S. Lazio – the most expensive club on Earth – before their 1999 Cup-Winners' Cup win.

Real Madrid have won the competition more than any other club. The last time was in 1998.

midfielders of the quality of Ivan de la Peña, Pavel Nedved and Dejan Stankovic. They will take a lot of stopping and should qualify from their group which also comprises Bayer Leverkusen, Dynamo Kiev and NK Maribor.

AC Milan, by their own high standards, hit a slump over the last two years but they recovered magnificently last season to win the Italian League and with players of the calibre of Andriy Shevchenko, Oliver Bierhoff and captain Paolo Maldini, they are ready to make a huge impact this season. The San Siro stadium will be bursting to the seams when Chelsea, Galatasaray and Hertha Berlin come calling and the AC fans will expect nothing less than qualification for the last four.

Whenever favourites for the European Cup are considered, Spanish giants Real Madrid are never far away. Their record is second to none and in recent years, their team has begun to recapture the glories of those of the 1950s and 60s. They will not be far away.

KEY PLAYERS

Real Madrid

Nikolas Anelka: The former Arsenal player might be moody and controversial, but put the ball in front of him and his pace will take him away from defenders. Put it in front of his left foot and he'll put it behind a goalkeeper. Real have been criticised for spending £21 million but if the sulky Anelka takes them to the final, he will have been worth every penny.

S.S. Lazio

Ivan de la Peña: The little Spaniard has never really fulfilled the potential he had as a teenager with Barcelona but the move to Italy could be the making of the midfielder. With great vision and passing ability, de la Peña will be pulling all the strings from the middle of the park and with the quality of strikers ahead of him, he shouldn't fail to impress.

FC HAKA 1   4 RANGERS

match highlights

Champions League 2nd Qualifying Round
1st Leg   28 July 1999
Attendance: 3,341
Referee: V Hrinak (Slovakia)

FC HAKA

Vilnrotter
Penttila
Karjalainen
Rasanen
Ivanov
Hyokyvarra
Reynders
Popovitch
Savolienan
Wilson
Niemi 51

substitutes
Nyyssonen
Okkonen
Pasanen
Rantala
Toivonen
Torkkeli

RANGERS

Klos
Adamczuk
Moore
Amoruso 18
Numan
Ferguson
Reyna (Nicholson 69)
Van Bronckhorst (Albertz 80)
Mols 28, 42
Wallace (Johansson 70)
McCann

substitutes
Albertz
Amato
Johansson
Nicholson 85
Niemi
Vidmar
Wilson

Recent signing from Utrecht Michael Mols became an instant hero with the Rangers fans on his competitive debut, by scoring two excellent goals and setting up a third which helped the club cruise on to a comfortable win over the Finnish Champions. Rangers were already a goal up after Amoruso's opener in the 18th minute when, in the 28th minute, Mols scored for his first competitive Rangers goal. Then the Dutchman seemed to create time and space for himself when he collected a pass from Neil McCann on the corner of the penalty box before powering the ball past Andras Vilnrotter in the Haka goal; it was not long before the half-time break and he had effectively finished the whole two-leg tie in the first half of the first match.

A lapse of concentration in the Rangers defence allowed Jarri Niemi to pull one back for Haka with a header six minutes after the break, but the visitors from Scotland never looked even close to losing control of the match. Three times Mols had the chance to complete his hat-trick but on each occasion the ball didn't quite fall for him.

Five minutes before the end, substitute Barry Nicholson – on for US international captain Claudio Reyna – rifled the ball into the net after a goalmouth scramble to make it 4-1 to Rangers. Already minds were turning to a re-match with old Italian adversaries Parma in the next round, rather than the replay against Haka that Rangers had to play first, only seven days later. New boy Mols had shown that he was capable of scoring at will, albeit against a team of Haka's somewhat lowly standing.

Michael Mols scores his first Rangers goal – in his first competitive game.

RANGERS 3 0 FC HAKA

match highlights

**Champions League 2nd Qualifying Round
2nd Leg 4 August 1999
Attendance: 50,000
Referee: L Pucek (Poland)**

Rangers went through the formality of their second leg against Haka, and as expected got through to the next round and a tie against Parma after a 3-0 victory. With a 4-1 advantage from the first game, Rangers manager Dick Advocaat was more concerned that he didn't reveal too much of his hand to the spies from Parma who were in the crowd, rather than worried about the Finns.

Michael Mols almost got his first goal at Ibrox after just three minutes, but it was ruled out for offside. Instead he was the provider when a neat flick from him found Rod Wallace who put Rangers ahead. After 27 minutes the tie was completely finished: Mols turned exquisitely in the penalty area but his shot was turned away for a corner. Van Bronckhorst took it, and his inswinger was headed into the net by Rangers' own Flying Finn Jonatan Johansson.

Their work complete, Rangers cantered through the rest of the game, but were unfortunate not to add more goals to their tally. Mols put Albertz in the clear just eight minutes later but the German could only find the side netting from 12 yards out. Minds seemed to be turning to the Parma match, and if that was the case Gabriel Amato staked his claim for a place in the team against them when he headed in a Darius Adamczuk cross for Rangers' third in the 65th minute.

Dick Advocaat said: 'There was some excellent movement and if we had scored three or four goals more the feeling would have been much better. We scored two quality goals and at times our one touch football was excellent. But there is still a lot to do and plenty of improvement to be made.'

RANGERS

Klos
Adamczuk
Moore
Amoruso
Numan (Vidmar 39)
Ferguson (Nicholson 71)
Johansson 28
Van Bronckhorst
Mols (Amato 46)
Wallace 15
Albertz

substitutes
Amato 66
Nicholson
Niemi
Vidmar
Wilson

FC HAKA

Vilnrotter
Penttila
Karjalainen
Rasanen (Savolianan 61)
Ivanov (Nyyssonen 55)
Reynders
Popovitch
Rantala
Wilson
Okkonen (Torkelli 71)
Niemi

substitutes
Nyyssonen
Salli
Savolianan
Toivonen
Torkelli
Pasanen

Gabriel Amato heads in goal number three on a night of European success.

RANGERS 2 0 PARMA

Champions League 3rd Qualifying Round
1st Leg 11 August 1999
Attendance: 49,263
Referee: J Garcia Aranda (Spain)

RANGERS

Klos
Porrini ■
Moore
Amoruso ■
Vidmar 33 (Albertz 55)
B Ferguson
Van Bronckhorst
Reyna 75
Mols
Wallace
McCann

substitutes
Adamczuk
Albertz ■
Amato
Johansson
McInnes
Niemi
Wilson

PARMA

Buffon
Sartor
Baggio (Fuser 60)
Ortega (Torrisi 37)
Boghossian
Cannavaro ■ ■
Di Vaio (Stanic 80)
Thuram
Serena
Vanoli ■
Walem

substitutes
Bennarivo
Breda
Fuser
Micillo
Montana
Stanic
Torrisi

match highlights

From start to finish Rangers tore at the Italian side and gained revenge for last season's defeat in the UEFA Cup. After just 40 seconds Rod Wallace broke away from his marker to get on the end of a cross from Giovanni van Bronckhorst, but he slipped his shot just wide. Parma were having difficulty adjusting to the pace of the game and started getting physical. After 15 minutes Fabio Cannavaro was booked for a late challenge and just 11 minutes later he received a second yellow card for another bookable offence and was sent off.

The home side raised the tempo even further, and Italian goalkeeper Gianluigi Buffon pulled off a great save from Claudio Reyna after a sweeping move involving Wallace and Neil McCann put him in the clear. But then the breakthrough came, and the man who provided it was one who wouldn't have been on the field if Arthur Numan had been fit: Tony Vidmar. A superb pass from McCann found Vidmar in the clear on the left. He stepped inside Antonio Bennarivo and rifled the ball high past Buffon.

Parma seemed to panic and coach Alberto Malesani took off £12 million Argentinian midfielder Ariel Ortega to replace him with Italian defender Torrisi. Ten minutes into the second half, and Tony Vidmar came off to a standing ovation, to be replaced by Jorg Albertz. The German's first moment of note was when he was controversially booked for diving when it seemed Rangers should have been given a penalty as Buffon sent him flying.

The tie turned in a five minute spell 20 minutes before the end. Parma were denied an equaliser when Stefan Klos pulled off a remarkable save. Rangers were inspired and crucially responded to the threat with a second goal. A pass from Wallace found McCann six yards from goal, and he laid the ball back into the path of Reyna who fired a shot through the packed area and into the net. In the last quarter of an hour both Wallace and van Bronckhorst missed good chances. Nonetheless Rangers had pulled off a remarkable result and had the kind of scoreline which gave Advocaat's team real hope of getting through to the Champions League at their first attempt.

Claudio Reyna celebrates a superb second goal, late in the game.

PARMA 1 0 RANGERS

match highlights

**Champions League 3rd Qualifying Round
2nd Leg 25 August 1999
Attendance: 29,000
Referee: K-E Nilsson (Sweden)**

The defending was dogged and desperate at times, but Rangers managed to hold on to their aggregate lead over Parma and qualified for the Champions League at the expense of the UEFA Cup holders.

It was a happy return to the Ennio Tardini Stadium for the Ibrox side, despite suffering their first defeat of the season. Less than ten months previously Rangers had been beaten 3-1 there to be eliminated from the UEFA Cup. This time Rangers did enough to edge out the Italian favourites and show just how much they have progressed in that time.

Dick Advocaat's tactics were always going to be to hold on to what he had – that hard won two-goal advantage from the first leg. He moved to a 3-5-2 formation, using Darius Adamczuk and Tony Vidmar wide in midfield to stem the flow of Parma's attacks down the flanks. Those tactics worked even if Rangers played well below their best. The Scottish champions were always on the back foot in the first half and couldn't keep possession; they nearly lost a goal as early as the fifth minute when Diego Fuser powered through the defence to set up Paulo Vanoli with a chance but Adamczuk, tracking back, did enough to put him off and he shot wildly over. Lionel Charbonnier was soon to be tested and produced two magnificent diving saves as Ariel Ortega bent in a couple of free-kicks.

Rangers were forced to defend deep and only threatened just before half-time when Tony Vidmar broke free. They had more chances in the second half though, first when Buffon produced a marvellous diving save to push away a Rod Wallace header after 48 minutes, and later when a 20-yard shot from Vidmar came back off the post. In the intense atmosphere Parma stepped up the pace and got a breakthrough when Charbonnier allowed a free-kick from Johan Walem to slip into the net when it had looked as though he had smothered the ball. That set up a nerve-racking last 20 minutes, but Charbonnier rediscovered his composure and the Rangers defence held their discipline to deny the Italians and claim a place amongst Europe's elite in the Champions League.

PARMA

Buffon
▌ Torrisi
Thuram
Lassissi
Fuser
Baggio
Boghossian (Walem 64)
Vanoli (Serena 78)
Ortega
Di Vaio (Stanic 63)
Crespo

substitutes
Bennarivo
Breda
Maini
Micillo
Serena
Stanic
Walem 68

RANGERS

Charbonnier
Porrini
▌ Amoruso
Moore
Adamczuk (Hendry 82)
Reyna
B Ferguson (Albertz 72)
Van Bronckhorst
Vidmar
Mols
▌ Wallace (McCann 60)

substitutes
Albertz
Amato
I Ferguson
Hendry
Johansson
McCann
Niemi

Despite losing the match, the Gers had a lot to celebrate – qualification for Europe's top club competition.

FIXTURES 1999-2000

1999

Date	Opponent	Venue	Competition
July			
28	FC Haka	A	UEFA Champions League 2nd Qualifying Round 1st Leg
31	Kilmarnock	H	Scottish Premier League
August			
4	FC Haka	H	UEFA Champions League 2nd Qualifying Round 2nd Leg
7	Heart of Midlothian	A	Scottish Premier League
11	Parma	H	UEFA Champions League 3rd Qualifying Round 1st Leg
15	Motherwell	H	Scottish Premier League
21	Dundee United	H	Scottish Premier League
25	Parma	A	UEFA Champions League 3rd Qualifying Round 2nd Leg
28	Hibernian	A	Scottish Premier League
September			
11	Aberdeen	H	Scottish Premier League
15	Valencia	A	UEFA Champions League
18	Celtic	A	Scottish Premier League
21	Bayern Munich	H	UEFA Champions League
25	St Johnstone	H	Scottish Premier League
28	PSV Eindhoven	A	UEFA Champions League
October			
2	Dundee	A	Scottish Premier League
12	Dunfermline	H	Scottish League Cup Round 3
16	Kilmarnock	A	Scottish Premier League
20	PSV Eindhoven	H	UEFA Champions League
23	Heart of Midlothian	H	Scottish Premier League
26	Valencia	H	UEFA Champions League
30	Aberdeen	A	Scottish Premier League
November			
3	Bayern Munich	H	UEFA Champions League
7	Celtic	H	Scottish Premier League
13	Dundee United	A	Scottish Premier League
20	Hibernian	H	Scottish Premier League
23			UEFA Champions League 2nd Group Stage
27	Dundee	H	Scottish Premier League
30			Scottish League Cup Round 4
December			
4	St Johnstone	A	Scottish Premier League
8			UEFA Champions League 2nd Group Stage
11	Kilmarnock	H	Scottish Premier League/Scottish Cup Round 1
18	Motherwell	A	Scottish Premier League
27	Celtic	A	Scottish Premier League

2000

Date	Opponent	Venue	Competition
January			
8			Scottish Cup Round 2
22	Aberdeen	H	Scottish Premier League
29			Scottish Cup Round 3
February			
5	Hibernian	A	Scottish Premier League
12	Dundee United	H	Scottish Premier League
19			Scottish Cup Round 4
26	Dundee	A	Scottish Premier League
29			UEFA Champions League 2nd Group Stage
March			
4	St Johnstone	H	Scottish Premier League
7			UEFA Champions League 2nd Group Stage
11	Heart of Midlothian	A	Scottish Premier League/Scottish Cup Round 5
14			UEFA Champions League 2nd Group Stage
18	Motherwell	H	Scottish Premier League
19			Scottish League Cup Final
21			UEFA Champions League 2nd Group Stage
26	Celtic	H	Scottish Premier League
April			
1	Aberdeen	A	Scottish Premier League
4			UEFA Champions League Quarter-final
8	Hibernian	H	Scottish Premier League/Scottish Cup Semi-final
15	Dundee United	A	Scottish Premier League
18			UEFA Champions League Quarter-final
22	St Johnstone	A	Scottish Premier League
29	Dundee	H	Scottish Premier League
May			
2			UEFA Champions League Semi-final
6	Kilmarnock	A	Scottish Premier League
9			UEFA Champions League Semi-final
13	Heart of Midlothian	H	Scottish Premier League
21	Motherwell	A	Scottish Premier League
24			UEFA Champions League Final
27			Scottish FA Cup Final

BUYING YOUR TICKETS & THE TEDDY BEARS CLUB

BUYING YOUR TICKETS

Subject to availability, tickets can be purchased in advance for any home game (apart from those against Celtic FC) in the following manner:

1 Submitting a home match application form (obtainable from the Ticket Centre) along with a cheque, postal order or credit/debit card details. Applications should be sent to The Ticket Centre, Edmiston House, 100 Edmiston Drive, Glasgow, G51 2YX at least three weeks in advance of the chosen game. Please do not send cash.

2 Calling the ticket hotline on 0870 600 1993 between 10am and 7pm on weekdays. Lines will be open for sale of tickets approximately 16 days before the game. You can pay by Access, Visa, MasterCard, Eurocard, Switch and Delta.

3 Calling at the Ticket Centre, Ibrox Stadium. Tickets are normally on sale two weeks prior to the game.

A limited number of season tickets are available throughout the year. Please call 0870 600 1993 for more information or if you would like to join the season ticket waiting list.

GETTING IN TOUCH

You will find the following telephone numbers useful should you wish to contact Rangers FC:

CLUBCALL	**0891 121 555**
COMMERCIAL	**0870 600 1899**
FAX ENQUIRIES	**0870 600 1978**
HOSPITALITY	**0870 600 1964**
TEDDY BEARS CLUB	**0870 600 1972**
TICKETS	**0870 600 1993**
RETAIL AND MAIL ORDER	**0990 99 1997**

and don't forget to visit our website: www.rangers.co.uk

THE TEDDY BEARS CLUB

The Teddy Bears Club is the official young supporters club for Rangers FC. It is for fans up to the age of 16, and we are proud to know that it is the second biggest young supporters club in the UK, with more than 13,000 members. Only Teddy Bears Club members can get to be matchday mascots: they are picked at random for every game at Ibrox.

Teddy Bears Club members receive the following:

• An official Teddy Bears Club contract from manager Dick Advocaat
• Rangers scarf
• Rangers autograph book
• Rangers branded skip cap
• Broxi Bear curly straw
• Membership card
• Newsletter exclusive to club members three times a year
• Exclusive birthday card
• 10 per cent off everything in Rangers Shops as well as great offers and savings in Teddy Bears Club appointed outlets
• Competitions to win tickets, special prizes and the chance to meet the players

Call 0870 600 1972 for information on how to join

SUPPORTERS' CLUBS

SCOTLAND

AIRDRIE VICTORIA RSC
Mr James McDowell
42 Nicol Street
Airdrie
Lanarkshire ML6 6HJ

ALLANTON LOYAL SC
Mr James Armit
51 Murdostoun View
Newmains
Lanarkshire ML2 9HD

ALLOA ROYAL BLUE RSC
Mrs Christina Bateman
4 Keverkae
Alloa
Clackmannanshire FK10 1QS

ALLYS CHOSEN FEW RSC
Mr Ian Tweddle
77 Lairhills Road
The Murray
Glasgow
Lanarkshire G75 0LH

ALVA & DISTRICT RSC
Mr John McLaren Talbot
13 Dunmar Crescent
Alloa
Clackmannanshire FK10 2EJ

ANNFIELD RSC
Mrs M Wilson
127 Whitburn Street
Glasgow
Lanarkshire G32 6RD

ANNIESLAND RSC
Mr Robert McFarlane
66 Sutcliffe Road
Glasgow
Lanarkshire G13 1AQ

ARDROSSAN & DALRY RSC
Mr Harry Herd
6 Alloway Place
Ardrossan
Ayrshire KA22 7HU

ARMADALE RSC
Mr Colin Cunningham
7 Earls Place
Fauldhouse
West Lothian EH47 9EB

ARMADALE IBROX RSC
Mr Albert Valentine
15 Glenside Gardens
Armadale
West Lothian EH48 3RA

ARROCHAR RSC
Mr Robert R Fulton
10 Hayes Grove
Sutherland Gardens
Alexandria G83 0UX

AUCHINLECK & DIST. RSC
Mr William Rowan
34 Greenside Place
Coal Road
Auchinleck
Ayrshire KA18 2AH

AYR & DIST. RSC
Mrs Nan Paterson
52 Ladywell Road
Maybole
Ayrshire KA19 7BE

ALLOWAY LOYAL
Mr Allan Low
2 Barnford Crescent
Alloway
Ayr
Ayrshire KA7 4UP

AM POL RSC
Mr John Millar
7 Makbrar Place
Dumfries
Dumfriesshire DG1 4BD

APC RANGERS
Mr Graham McEwan
228 Crofthill Road
Croftfoot
Glasgow G44 5NN

ABERLOUR BEARS RSC
Mr Peter Kelman
25 Springfield Drive
New Elgin
Moray IV30 1XZ

ALNESS DINGWALL TRUE BLUES RSC
Mr George Reid
85 Shillinghill
Alness
Rosshire IV17 0TA

ARBROATH SMOKIE BEARS RSC
Mr James Smith Jnr
100 Bellevue Gardens
Arbroath
Angus DD1 5BQ

LORENZO AMORUSO No.3 LOYAL
Mr John Rossi
35 Renshaw Drive
Hillington
Glasgow G52 2JN

BAILLIESTON TRUE BLUES
Mr A McShannon
14 Richardson Avenue
Hurlford
Kilmarnock KA1 5DA

BALLINGRY LOYAL RSC
Mr David Wilson
5 King Street
Cowdenbeath
Fife KY4 9DU

BATHGATE & DISTRICT RSC
Mr Angus McLeod
133 Deanswood Park
Deans
Livingston EH54 8NZ

BEITH SARACEN RSC
Mr John Stirrat
4 Grahamfield Place
Beith
Ayrshire KA15 1AY

BELLSHILL CHOSEN FEW RSC
Mr Gordon Mckay
17 Raith Drive
Bellshill
Lanarkshire ML4 2JF

BELLSHILL & DISTRICT
Mr William Clowes
13 Sweethill Walk
Bellshill ML4 1TE

BENTS & DIST. RSC
Mr Ian Watson
115 The Glebe
West Calder
West Lothian EH55 8BW

BLUE BEAR RSC
Mr Joseph Yates
24 Caroline Crescent
Alva
Clamannanshire FK12 5BT

BLUES BROTHERS
Mr John McLellan
26 Stewartville Street
Partick
Glasgow GL11 5PJ

BLUES AND ROYALS DENNY
Mrs Lorna Anderson
2 Hillhouse Road
Denny
Stirlingshire FK6 5PG

BO'NESS TRUE BLUES RSC
Mr David Leith
37 Woodlands Drive
Bo'ness
West Lothian EH51 0NT

BRIDGE OF WEIR DIST. RSC
Yvonne Brown
31 Gorse Crescent
Bridge of Weir
Renfrewshire PA11 3LX

BRIDGEND & DIST. TRUE BLUES RSC
Mr Kenneth L Lindsay
55 Barons Hill Avenue
Linlithgow
West Lothian EH49 7JQ

BRIDGETON CHOSEN FEW RSC
Mrs Annette Fowler
72 Garthland Drive
Cranhill
Glasgow G31 3RD

BRIDGETON LOYAL RSC
Mr James McManus
27 Bernard Terrace
House 9
Bridgeton
Glasgow G40 3BD

BRIDGETON 5-1
Mr John McIntyre
11 Bernard Path
Bridgeton
Glasgow G40 3BE

BRISTOL BAR LOYAL RSC
Mr Joseph Nixon (Jnr)
562 Gallowgate
Haghill
Glasgow G40 2PA

BROTHERS IN BLUE RSC
Mr Alan Porter
120 Eastwood Avenue
Glasgow
Lanarkshire G41 3RT

BROWN STREET RSC
Mrs Jaqueline Stevely
3 The Old School
Lintwhite Crescent
Bridge of Weir
Renfrewshire PA11 3LJ

BROXBURN RSC
Mr Murray McLaren
21 Society Road
South Queensferry
West Lothian EH30 9XP

BUCKHAVEN & METHIL RSC
Ms Hayley Wilson
3b Viewforth Square
Leven
Fife KY8 4PQ

BURNBANK RSC
Mr John Rankin
42 Dunlin
Stewartfield
East Kilbride
Lanarkshire G14 4RX

BARNMULLOCH RANGERS
Mr David Hain
256 Rye Road
Barmulloch
Glasgow G21 3JR

BRIDGE STREET LINWOOD
Mr Colin Craig
60B Kilbrennan Road
Linwood
Paisley
Renfrewshire PA3 3RD

BROXI BEAR LOYAL RSC
Mr Scott Kerr
52 Bank Street
Paisley Renfrewshire PA1 1LR

BLANTYRE RSC
Mr Scott McMillan
42 Farm Road
Blantyre
Glasgow G72 9DT

BELLFIED RSC
Mr Graeme Scott
14 Lomond Road
Kilmarnock
Ayrshire KA1 3SH

CALDERWOOD RSC
Mr Thomas Clark
1 Waverely Terrace
High Blantyre
Lanarkshire G72 0HN

CALEDONIAN RSC
Mr David Whitecross
Laighbent Cottage
High Bent Road
Strathaven
Lanarkshire ML10 6QD

CAMBUSLANG LOYAL RSC
Mr Grant Wilson
8 Stanford Hall
Main Street
Cambuslang
Glasgow G72 7HG

CAMBUSLANG NO SURRENDER RSC
Mr Garry Lynch
29 Gilbertfield Road
Cambuslang
Glasgow G72 8XB

CAMELON RSC
Mr Gordon Duncan
Masonic Arms
224 Glasgow Road
Longcroft
Stirlingshire FK4 1QP

CAMERON HOUSE RSC
Mr Andrew Moore (Jnr)
28 Abbeylands Road
Faifley
Clydebank
Glasgow G81 5LE

CAMERON LOYAL RSC
Mr W MacFarlane
17 Dunglass Avenue
Glasgow
Lanarkshire G14 9DX

CAMPSIE LOYAL
Mr Brian Marshall
13 Service Street
Lennoxtown
Glasgow G65 7JW

CARDENDEN LOYAL RSC
Mr James MacDonald
113 Denfield Avenue
Cardenden
Lochgelly
Fife KY5 0BX

CARLUKE YOUNG LOYALISTS RSC
Mr James Smith
40 Glenmavis Crescent
Carluke
Lanarkshire ML8 4JL

CARMYLE RSC
Mr James Buchanan
156 Estate Road
Carmyle
Glasgow
Lanarkshire G32 8AQ

CARSON STAR RSC
Mr Neil Findlay
62 Craigie Road
Ayr
Ayrshire KA8 0HA

CASTLE ST. LOYAL PAISLEY RSC
Mr Brian Donaghy
6 Hollows Avenue
Foxbar
Paisley
Renfrewshire PA2 0RB

CAVENDISH RSC
Mr John Montgomery
37 Ellangowan Road
Glasgow
Lanarkshire G41 3SZ

CENTRAL FIFE RSC
Mr Ross Blyth
48 Middlebank Street
Rosyth
Fife KY11 2NY

CLACHAN CAR RSC
Mr Iain MacIver
41 Allan Park
Kirkliston
West Lothian EH29 9HA

JIMMY CLARK LOYAL RSC
Mr Robert Ferguson
Flat 11
37 Bathgate Street
Glasgow
Lanarkshire G31 1DZ

CLARKSTON RSC
Mr Alan Park
50 Woodyett road
Busby
Glasgow
Lanarkshire G76 8SB

CLYDEBANK LOYAL RSC
Mr Peter Greenlees
120 Dickens Avenue
Clydebank
Glasgow G81 3EP

COATBRIDGE RSC
Mr David Hulme
7 Parkview Drive
Coatbridge ML5 1NL

CONDORRAT RSC
Mr W Anderson
101 Cardowan Road
Stepps
Glasgow G33 6AW

CRIEFF TRUE BLUES
Mr Raymond Cramb
22 Alligan Crescent
Crieff
Perthshire PH7 3JT

CROSS TAVERN RSC
Mr John Caskie
17 Gardner Crescent
Whitburn
Bathgate
West Lothian EH47 0PF

CROWN BAR BELLSHILL
Mr Ian Phillips
16 Bannockburn Place
New Stevenson
Lanarkshire ML1 4DE

CUMBERNAULD CARBRAIN RSC
Mr David Carslaw
11 Edenside
Cumbernauld
Glasgow
Lanarkshire G68 0ER

CUMNOCK TRUE BLUES
Mr Derek Walker
118 Coyle Avenue
Drongan
Ayrshire KA6 7DW

CHASE RSC
Mr Ingles
29 Woodstock Avenue
Kirkintilloch
Glasgow G66 3RS

CALDERBANK TRUE BLUES RSC
Mr Angus Cameron
1 Crowood Crescent
Calderbank
By Airdrie
Lanarkshire ML6 9TA

CHOSEN FEW RSC
Ms Jacqueline Wilson
3 Park Avenue
Croftfoot
Glasgow G73 2QG

CONDORRAT CHOSEN FEW
Mr Ian Marshall
85 Montrose Gardens
Kilsyth
Glasgow
Lanarkshire G65 9BQ

COALBURN RSC
Mr James Graham
65 School Road
Coalburn ML11 0LR

DALBEATTIE RSC
Mr R Henderson
7 Craignair View
DALBEATTIE
Kirkcudbrightshire DG5 EG

DALMARNOCK LOYAL RSC
Mr Robert Forrester
145 Greenhead Street
Glasgow
Lanarkshire G40 1HU

DENNISTOUN LOYAL RSC
Miss Lorraine Ramsay
145 Roslea Drive
Dinnistoun
Glasgow
Lanarkshire G31 2RZ

DENNY & DIST. RSC
Mr Charles Nelson
9 Randolph Gardens
Denny
Stirlingshire FK6 5DB

DOUBLE FIVE LOYAL
Mr David Stewart
26 Crofters Gate
East Whitburn
West Lothian EH47 8ER

DRUMCHAPEL LOYAL RSC
Mr John Ross
42 Kiniver Drive
Blairdardie
Glasgow G15 6RF

DRUMRY RSC
Mr Robert Clinton
286 Duntocher Road
Clydebank
Glasgow G81 3JH

DUMBARTON LOYAL RSC
Mr David Cameron
14a Wallace Street
Dumbarton
Dumbartonshire G82 1HJ

DUNFERMLINE LOYAL RSC
Mr Bruce McAuliffe
52 Lilac Grove
Dunfermline
Fife KY11 8AP

IAN DURRANT FOLLOW FOLLOW
Mr D Wilson
10 Gartshore Gardens
Blackwood
Cumbernauld G68 9NH

EAST KILBRIDE RSC
Mr Arthur Bishop
28 Chestnut Crescent
Greenhills
East Kilbride G75 9EL

EASTERHOUSE LOYAL RSC
Mr R Hendry
23 Dunskaith Street
Easterhouse
Glasgow G34 0AN

EDINBURGH JARDINE RSC
Mr S Richardson
44 Queen Margaret Close
Edinburgh
Midlothian EH10 7EE

EDDLEWOOD RSC
Mr W Kane
c/o 18 Tay Gardens
Woodhead
Hamilton
Lanarkshire ML3 8TG

ELLANGOWAN RSC
Mr Iain Sinclair
46 Keystone Avenue
Milngavie Glasgow
Lanarkshire G62 6HZ

ERSKINE LOYAL RSC
Mr Graham Thomson
24 Parksail
Parkmains
Erskine PA8 7HT

EYEMOUTH RSC
Mr Iain Turnbull
32 The Avenue
Eyemouth TD1X 5EB

FALLIN RSC
Mr Archie Bone
62 King Street
Fallin
Stirling
Stirlingshire FK7 7JY

DUNCAN FERGUSON LOYAL
Mr John McCallum
30 Borestone Place
St Ninians
Stirling
Stirlingshire FK7 0PP

FERNILL LOYAL RSC
Mr George Lindsay
38 Morar Drive
Rutherglen
Glasgow
Lanarkshire G73 4DJ

FIFE LOYAL RSC
Mr John G King
23 Warout road
Glenrothes
Fife KY7 4JJ

FIFE RED, WHITE & BLUES RSC
Mr John White
Marven
Oakum Bay
Newmills
Fife KY12 8TD

FORFAR QUEEN STREET
Mr Alistair Gourlay
29 Brechin Road
Forfar
Angus DD8 3JR

FORT WILLIAM RSC
Mr Colin Pinkett
73 Lochaber Road
Fort William
Inverness-Shire PH33 6TX

FORTH RANGERS RSC
Mr Derek Roberts
6 Birniehall
Forth
Lanark ML11 8DF

FRASERBURGH LOYAL RSC
Mr John Soutar
22 Thompson Terrace
Fraserburgh
Aberdeenshire AB43 9NY

FULWOOD LOYAL RSC
Mr George Thomson
31 Glentyan Avenue
Kilbarchan
Johnstone
Renfrewshire PA10 2JU

FORFAR TRUE BLUES
Mrs Lesley Lawreson
38 Glenclova Terrace
Forfar
Angus DD8 1NS

FIRST PARANOID RSC
Mr Dean Rolland
36 Third Avenue
Millerston
Glasgow G33 6JU

FERGIE LOYAL RSC
Mr John Brodie
2 Armadale Place
Dennistoun
Glasgow
Lanarkshire G31 3ES

GABLE ENDER RANGERS RSC
Mr Frank G Wood
25 Newmanswalls Avenue
Montrose
Angus DD10 9DD

GALSTON & DISTRICT
Mr A J Brown
3H Isles Street
Newmilns
Ayrshire KA16 9DP

GARTCOSH RSC
Mr Stephen Weir
7 Glenburn Avenue
Moodiesburn
Glasgow G69 0BS

GLENMAVIS RSC
Mr Les Stanners
49 Monkland Street
Airdrie
Lanarkshire ML6 9NJ

GILMOUR FRENCH RSC
Ms Elizabeth Smith
30 Milnwood Court
Glenrothes
Fife KY6 2PD

GOWANBRAE RSC
Mr Alex Robertson
35 Elswick Drive
Caldercruix
Airdrie ML6 7QW

GREENGAIRS LOYAL RSC
Mr Douglas Ward
166 Luing
Airdrie
Lanarkshire ML6 8EE

GREENOCK RSC
Mr Colin Campbell
17E Grey Place
Greenock
Renfrewshire PA15 1FA

GLENMAVIS 2000
Mr William Clark
22 Meldrum Mains
Glenmavis
Airdrie ML6 0QG

GRATTUSO LOYAL RSC
Mr Richard Welsh
24 Carse View
Airth
Falkirk FK2 8NY

GALASHIELS No. 1 RSC
Mr Ian Campbell
22 Galapark Gardens
Galashiels TD1 1ES

GLENNY LOYAL RSC
Mr Robert Blair
7 Earnview Place
Comrie
Perthshire PA7

HADDINGTON & DISTRICT RSC
Mr Tom Trotter
12 Amisfield Place
Haddington
East Lothian EH41 4NG

HARTHILL RSC
Mr William Pringle
7 Boghead Crescent
Falside
Bathgate
West Lothian EH48 2DT

HAWICK RSC
Mr Ewan Lawrence
2 Glebe Mill Street
Hawick
Roxburghshire TD9 9QD

HIGH BLANTYRE RSC
Mr David McKean
10 Mavis Bank
High Blantyre
Lanarkshire G72 0RT

HIGHLAND NO. 1 SC
Mr Scott Brown
2 Craigard Place
Inverness
Inverness-Shire IV3 6PR

HILLHOUSE RSC
Mr Derek Rodger
17 Dunscore Brae
Earnock
Hamilton ML3 9DH

HILLINGTON LOYAL
Mr Jim Hutton
182 Hillington Road South
Hillington
Glasgow G52 2AU

HOLYTOWN RSC
Ms Marion Rodger
2 Wrangholm Crescent
New Stevenson
Motherwell ML1 4EP

HOLYTOWN LOYAL RSC
Mr Jim McNair
14 Whitelaw Crescent
Mossend
Bellshill
Lanarkshire ML4 2RG

HOLYTOWN MASONIC ARMS
Mr Ian Camberon
168 Burnhead Street
Viewpark
Uddingston
Lanarkshire G71 5AS

HORSESHOE BAR
Mr I Paterson
28 Chapelhill
Clackmannan
Clackmannanshire FK10 4JP

HONEST TOUN LOYAL
Mr John Frame
16 Marshall Street
Edinburgh EH8 9BU

HALIFAX LOYAL RSC
Mr Adrian Marsden
25 Woodbrook Avenue
Halifax
Yorkshire HX2 8QE

HALFWAY TRUE BLUES RSC
Mr Stephen McIntyre
25 Bowmont Place
Cambuslang G72 7YJ

HIGHLANDER BARRY FERGUSON LOYAL
Mr Alexander Savill
c/o 104 Bruntsfield Avenue
South Nitshill
Glasgow G53 7BQ

IBROX 101 RSC
Mr William Duncan
1 South Park Avenue
Barrhead
Glasgow
Lanarkshire G78 1QF

INVERNESS TRUE BLUES RSC
Mr Roderick MacLean
2 Craig Phadrig Terrace
Lochalsh road
Inverness
Inverness-Shire IV3 8HR

IRVINE & DISTRICT RSC
Mr David MacDonald
5 Birkscairn Place
Irvine
Ayrshire KA11 1ED

ISLE OF SKYE LOYAL RSC
Mr Malcolm MacInnes
Shiloh
Upper Breakish
Isle of Skye IV42 8PY

IVY BANK NO SURRENDER RSC
Mr Gordon Rutherford
135 Brassey Street
Ruchill
Glasgow
Lanarkshire G20 9HN

IRVINES CHOSEN FEW
Mr Andy Frew
34 Crows Grove
Irvine
Ayrshire KA12 0XP

INTERNET LOYAL RSC
Mr Alan Rankin
78 Rosemount Street
Royston
Glasgow
Lanarkshire G21 2JY

JOHNSTONE RSC
Mr Ian MacPhee
3 Park Road
Johnstone
Renfrewshire PA5 8LT

JB RSC
Mr Garry Scott
15 Duntreath Gardens
Old Drumchapel
Glasgow
Dumbartonshire G15 6SH

KELSO LOYAL
Mr Stuart Douglas
4 Tanners Court
Kelso
Roxburghshire TD5 7NH

KENMURE RSC
Mr Ian Devine
108 Meiklerig Crescent
Glasgow
Lanarkshire G53 5UF

KILBIRNIE TOM FORSYTH RSC
Mr John McLean
54 Herriot Avenue
Kilbirnie
Ayrshire KA25 7JB

KILMARNOCK TEDDY BEARS RSC
Mr D A Gilchrist
46 East Park Drive
Kilmaurs
Ayrshire KA3 2QS

KILSYTH RSC
Mr Duncan Angus
60 Arden Grove
Kilsyth
Glasgow
Lanarkshire G65 9NU

KINGDOM TRUE BLUES RSC
Mr John Bean
16 Bickram Crescent
Comrie
Dunfermline
Fife KY12 9XL

KINGHORN & BURNTISLAND RSC
Mr James T Barn
Ladyburn Villa
Bruce Terrace
Burntisland
Fife KY3 9TH

KINGSPARK LOYAL RSC
Mr Cameron McGillvray
68 Ardmory Avenue
Old Toryglen
Glasgow
Lanarkshire G42 0BT

KINNING PARK LOYAL RSC
Mr S Daniels
7/4, 12 Swinton Place
Glasgow
Lanarkshire G52 2EA

KINROSS LOYAL RSC
Ms Heather Cowan
2 Princess Crescent
Freuchie
Glenrothes
Fife KY7 7HN

KIRKINTILLOCH RSC
Mr David Watson
122 Redbrae Road
Kirkintilloch
Glasgow
Lanarkshire G66 2DD

KIRKMUIRHILL RSC
Mr A Simpson
17 Bellfield Road
Coalburn
Lanark
Lanarkshire ML11 0LA

KIRKSHAWS RSC
Mr Edward Kyle
64 Kirkshaws Avenue
Coatbridge
Lanarkshire ML5 5BT

KIRKTON LOYAL RSC
Mr Douglas Selkirk
33 Townhill Road
Hamilton
Lanarkshire ML3 9UX

KYLE & DIST. RSC
Mr George Macrae
The Flat
The Butchers Shop
Kyle of Lochalsh
Ross-Shire IV40 8BT

ARCHIE KNOX LOYAL
Mr Stuart Newton
27 Cameron Knowe
Phipstoun
West Lothian EH49 6RL

KILBIRNIE RSC
Mr David Johnstone
42 Dennyholm Wynd
Kilbirnie
Ayrshire KA25 6HG

KEMLIN TRUE BLUES
Mr A Jackson
12 Wall Gardens
Camelon
Falkirk FK1 4HX

LARKFIELD LOYAL R.S.C.
Mr Alex Taggart
22 Bankfoot Road
Cardonald
Glasgow
Lanarkshire G52 2TE

LARKHALL & DIST. RSC
Mr Thomas McPhee
2 Croft Place
Larkhall
Lanarkshire ML 1BQ

LARKHALL LOYAL RSC
Mr Clarke Fortune
56 Raploch Road
Larkhall
Lanarkshire ML9 1AN

LARKHALL TRUE BLUES
Mr George Glen
Hawthorne Gardens
Larkhall
Lanarkshire ML9 2TD

LAURISTON LOYAL RSC
Mr S Bonsor
32c Richmond Walk
Aberdeen AB25 2YT

LAW LOYAL RSC
Mr John Corbett
7 Brownlee Road
Law
Carluke
Lanarkshire ML8 5JD

LETHAMHILL LOYAL RSC
Mr J Davidson
207 Warriston Street
Carntyne
Glasgow
Lanarkshire G33 2LE

LEVENSIDE RANGERS SC
Mr Nigel Patterson
24 Wades Road
Kinlochleven
Argyll PA40 4QX

LINLITHGOWBRIDGE LOYALS
Mr Peter Stevenson
17 Pentland Way
Grangemouth
Stirlingshire FK3 0EA

LINWOOD NO. 1. RSC
Mr Gordon Dinnie
63 Loanhead Avenue
Linwood
Renfrewshire PA3 3QP

LOCKERBIE LOYAL RSC
Mr Neil J Cameron
62 Bridge Street
Lockerbie
Dumfriesshire DG11 2HR

LANARK TRUE BLUES
Mr Tom Weir
16 Braedale road
Lanark
Lanarkshire ML11 7AN

LENZIE TRUE BLUES
Mr Colin Rankin
84 Boghead Road
Lenzie
Lanarkshire G66 4EN

BRIAN LAUDRUP LOYAL (BONHILL)
Mr William McLaren
23 First Avenue
Bonhill
Alexandria
Dunbartonshire G83 9BB

LANDSIDE LOYAL RSC
Mr Alan MacNeill
4 McGregoor Court
Hawthorn Grove
Cambuslang
Glasgow G78 7GD

LIVINGSTON SOUTH LOYAL RSC
Mr David Watt
40 Herald Rise
Dedridge
Livingston
West Lothian EH54 6JG

LINN 'O' DEE RSC
Mr Connor McGrath
3 Abercromby Drive
Bellgrove Court
Glasgow
Lanarkshire G40 2HW

LIVINGSTON STATION NO. 1 RSC
Mr Ryan Chapman
123 Harburn Avenue
Deans
Livingston
West Lothian EH54 8NL

LOTHIAN TRUE BLUES RSC
Mr Wallace Scobie
25 Dobbies Road
Bonnyrigg
Midlothian EH19 2BA

10 M
Mr Thomas McGhee
19 Sutherness Drive
Cranhill
Glasgow
Lanarkshire G33 3GA

STUART MCCALL GRAPES BAR LOYAL
Mr Malcolm MacPherson
220 Paisley Road West
Flat 1/2
Glasgow
Lanarkshire G51 1BU

**ALLY MCCOIST &
WEE DES LOYAL RSC**
Mrs Rose Belkevitz
8 Glem Dye
St Leonards
East Kilbride
Lanarkshire G74 3SS

MIDCALDER RSC
Mr Harry McNee
146 Barclay Way
Knightsridge
Livingston
West Lothian EH54 8HB

MILNGAVIE RSC
Mr Barry Lee
35 Graham Drive
Milngavie
Glasgow
Lanarkshire G62 7DY

MONTROSE RSC
Mr John Clark
46 Newmanswalls Avenue
Montrose
Angus DD10 9DD

MOTHERWELL TRUE BLUES
Mr Gavin Curwood
9 Barr Street
Motherwell
Lanarkshire ML1 1JA

MOUNT FLORIDA R.S.C.
Mr James McLean
74 Croftmont Avenue
Croftfoot
Glasgow
Lanarkshire G44 5LH

NEIL MURRAY RSC
Mr Alan Hill
13 Ochiltree Place
Kilmarnock
Ayrshire KA3 6FE

MEMORIES OF PARTICK LOYAL
Mr Ian Nicol
1559 Dumbarton Road
Scotstoun
Glasgow
Lanarkshire G14 9XF

MAYFIELD AND NEWTON GRANGE RSC
Mr Allan Morton
4 Bevan Road
Mayfield
Dalkeith
Midlothian EH22 5QE

MILLERSTON RSC
Mr David Thorn
25 Fourth Avenue
Millerston
Glasgow
Lanarkshire G33 6JY

MICHELLE LOYAL RSC
Mr James Gordon Donald
23 East Whitefield
Dunfermline KY12 0RH

NEIL MCCANN LOYAL RSC
Mr George McNee
1 Davidson Way
Knightsridge
Livingston
West Lothian EH54 8HG

NAIRN RSC
Mr Michael Stewart
16 Loch Avenue
Nairn
Morayshire IV12 4TF

NEW CUMNOCK AND DISTRICT RSC
Mr James Modrate
76E Afton Bridgend
New Cumnock
CUMNOCK
Ayrshire KA18 4JQ

NEW CUMBERNAULD LOYAL
Mr Robert Morris
35 Avon Street
Dunnipace
Denny
Stirlingshire FK6 6LD

NEW LIVINGSTON RSC
Mr Stephen Cosgrove
113 Huron Avenue
Howden
Livingston
West Lothian EH54 6LG

NEW TOWN RANGERS SC
Mr George Stirling
10D Elliot House
Burns Road
Cumbernauld
Lanarkshire G67 2AN

NEWMACHER RED WHITE & BLUE
Mr Charles Gaff
4 Midtan-g Bancs
Stonehaven AB39 2UJ

NEWMAINS RSC
Mr William Finnie
10 Mavisbank
Newmains
Wishaw
Lanarkshire ML2 9AH

NITH VALLEY RSC
Mr John Torrance
18 Queens Crescent
Sanquhar
Dumfriesshire DG4 6DW

NORTH CLYDE TEDDY BEARS RSC
Mr William Reid
233 Kinfauns Drive
Drumchapel
Glasgow
Lanarkshire G15 7BH

JOHN NIVEN EDINBURGH LOYAL
Mr Tony Haddow
50/6 North Fort Street
Edinburgh EH33 1AU

ORKNEY RSC
Mr Leonard Bain
17 Quoybank Place
Kirkwall
Orkney KW15 1ES

OLD MONKLAND LOYAL
Mr Fraser McDonald
18 Cadzow Crescent
Coatbridge
Lanarkshire ML5 5NY

OKEY DOKEY LOYAL
Mr Andrew Strawhorn
33 Glen Farrar Way
Meadowbrook
Kilmarnock
Ayrshire KA2 0LP

PARKVILLE RSC
Mr R Robertson
3 Sunnydale Drive
Blackridge
Bathgate
West Lothian EH48 TB

PARTICK LOYAL RSC
Miss E Macdonald
3 Palmer Avenue
Knightswood
Glasgow
Lanarkshire G13 2LL

PATNA TRUE BLUES RSC
Ms Angela Kennedy
12 Minnoch Road
Dalmellington
Ayrshire KA6 7SX

PERTH TRUE BLUES RSC
Mr Allan Melloy
116 Bute Drive
North Muirton
Perth
Perthshire PH1 3DA

PETERHEAD TRUE BLUES RSC
Mr William Stephen
Cedar Lea
18 Station Road
Longside
Peterhead AB42 4GR

PETERSHILL LOYAL RSC
Mr William Thompson
623 Hawthorn Street
Glasgow
Lanarkshire G22 6AZ

PLEAN RSC
Mr Alex Penman
28 Touchill Crescent
Plean Stirling
Stirlingshire FK7 8DX

POLMONT LOYAL RSC
Mr Robert Kennedy
64 College Crescent
Middlefield
Falkirk
Stirlingshire FK2 9HN

PORT GLASGOW GLEN RSC
Mr T Stirling
22 Bank Street
Greenock
Renfrewshire PA15 4PH

PRINCE HENRY RSC
Mr T Gentleman
1 Whyte Street
Harthill
Shotts
Lanarkshire ML7 5SP

QUEENZIEBURN RSC
Mr Graham Forsyth
65 Howe Road
Kilsyth Glasgow
Lanarkshire G65 0LW

QUEEN STREET TRUE BLUES
Mr Robert Gibbons
43 Torr Road
Bishopsbriggs
Glasgow
Lanarkshire G64 1XH

RANGERS POOLS
c/o Ticket Office
Edmiston House
100 Edmiston Drive
Ibrox
Glasgow G51 2YX

RENFREW LOYAL RSC
Mr John W Begg
52 Cramond Avenue
Renfrew
Renfrewshire PA4 0XG

ROCHSOLES LOYAL RSC
Mr Robert Murphy
6 Laggan Road
Burnfoot
Airdrie
Lanarkshire ML6 0LH

ROCHSOLLOCH RSC
Mr Gavin Dalzell
35 Crathie Drive
Glenmavis
Airdrie
Lanarkshire ML6 0NR

ROSEHALL RSC
Mr Alan Black
86 Blairhill Street
Coatbridge
Lanarkshire ML5 1PJ

BILLY RUSSELL MEMORIAL RSC
Mr John Goldie
3 Robert Knox Avenue
Tullibody
Alloa
Clackmannanshire K10 2UF

RAILWAY INN RSC
Mr David Park
21 High Burnside Avenue
Coatbridge
Lanarkshire ML5 1HZ

RUMOURS BAR RSC
Mr Graham Provan
7 Beechwood Grove
Barrhead
Glasgow
Lanarkshire G78 2JH

ROZENTAL LOYAL RSC
Mr Harry McCallum
42 Binniehill Road
Cumbernauld
Glasgow
Lanarkshire G68 9JJ

REDDING & WESTQUARTER RSC
Mr Kenneth Hollis
5 Valleyview Drive
Falkirk
Stirlingshire FK2 7JA

ROXI BEAR LOYAL
Mr Matt Donald
13 Raith Drive
Blackwood
Cumbernauld G68 9PE

SALUTATION RSC
Mr Alan Petrie
24a Easterbank
Forfar
Angus DD8 2BT

SELKIRK LOYAL RSC
Mr Ewan MacDougall
4 Elm Row
Selkirk
Selkirkshire TD7 4EU

SHOTTS RSC
Mr John Murphy
91 Bute Crescent
Dykehead
SHOTTS
Lanarkshire ML7 4JP

SILVER GLEN RSC
Mr Gary McCheyne
26 Johnstone Street
Alva
Clackmannanshire FK12 5AE

WATER SMITH HELENSBURGH LOYAL RSC
Mr Ian Devine
55 Dumbuie Avenue
Dumbarton
Dumbartonshire G82 2JH

GEORGE SOUTAR LOYAL RSC
Mr Thomas Green
74 Mahon Court
Moodiesburn
Glasgow
Lanarkshire G69 0QF

SPRINGBURN LOYAL RSC
Mr John Dryburgh
40 Carbisdale Street
Glasgow
Lanarkshire G22 6BU

SPRINGBURN TRUE BLUES RCS
Mr Samuel Watt
1/2 57 Laverockhall Street
Springburn
Glasgow
Lanarkshire G21 4AE

STENHOUSEMUIR & BAINSFORD T B'S
Mr Alistair Patterson
35 Lamond View
Stenhousemuir
Larbert
Stirlingshire FK5 3BW

STEVENSON RSC
Mr James Templeton
21 Crannog Way
Culzean park
Kilwinning
Ayrshire KA13 6NW

STEVENSON CROSS KEYS RSC
Mr R Beattie
20 Sommerville Drive
Stevenson
Syrshire KA20 3PA

JOHN STEVENSON JNR RSC
Mr James Barrie
69 Cornhill Drive
Coatbridge
Lanarkshire ML5 1RT

STEWARTON 'FOLLOW FOLLOW' RSC
Mr Barry Hay
8 Auchentiber Place
Kilmarock
Ayrshire KA3 6BG

STONEHOUSE RSC
Mr George Smith
6 Naismith Court
Stonehouse
Larkhall
Lanarkshire ML9 3HE

STRATHGRYFFE BRIDGE OF WEIR RSC
Mr Malcolm Brodie
Houston
Renfrewshire PA6 7NX

SALSBURGH TRUE BLUES RSC
Mr James MacDonald
22 Sighthill Terrace
Salsburgh
SHOTTS
Lanarkshire ML7 4NB

ST ANDREWS HOTEL RSC
Mr Angus Oakley
18 Fiddison Place
Prestwick
Ayrshire KA9 2TJ

SUNNYSIDE LOYAL RSC
Mr Douglas Hutton
33 Montgomery Avenue
Coatbridge
Lanarkshire ML5 1QR

SALTCOATS (MERMAID) RSC
Mr Michael Woods
10 Wheatley Road
Stevenston
Aryshire KA20 4EU

SHAWLANDS LOYAL
Mr Danny Fenn
28 Skirving Street
Shawlands
Glasgow G41 3AA

SCOTT LOYAL RSC
Mr Kenneth Scott
102 Sandy Road
Renfrew
Renfrewshire

TANNOCHSIDE RSC
Mr Graham Reid
40 Hamilton View
Uddngston
Glasgow
Lanarkshirev G71 6QA

MATT TAYLOR MEMORIAL RSC
Mrs Gayle Wilson
3 Tummel Green
East Mains
Glasgow
Lanarkshire G74 4AJ

THORNHILL LOYAL RSC
Mr Gordon Dunbar
Galabreck House
Galabreck Road
Thornhill
Dumfriesshire DG3 4LP

THORNLIEBANK TRUE BLUES RSC
Mr Tony Bellingham
49 Bonnyrigg Drive
Eastwood
Glasgow
Lanarkshire G43 1HP

TITWOOD RSC
Mr David Tennant
794 Polloksahws Road
Glasgow
Lanarkshire G41

TORRISDALE TRUE BLUES RSC
Mr Ian McGraw
85 Cartside Street
Langside Glasgow
Lanarkshire G42 9TJ

TORYGLEN TRUE BLUES RSC
Mr John Mitchell
9 Campsie View
Uddingston
Glasgow
Lanarkshire G71 6TZ

TOWNHEAD RSC
Mr John Buchanan
44 Banner Road
Glasgow
Lanarkshire G13 2HN

TUDOR LOYAL RSC
Mr Kenneth Speirs
64 Craigielinn Avenue
Glenburn
Paisley
Renfrewshire PA2 8QU

TOGIES TRUE BLUES RSC
Miss Pamela Watson
78 Church Place
Fauldhouse
Bathgate
West Lothian EH47 9HU

TOBY TRUE BLUES
Mr Richard Pollock
183 Millersneuk Crescent
Millerston
Glasgow
Lanarkshire G33 6PW

TAIL O'THE BANK RSC
Mr Raymond Williams
5 Burns Drive
Weymss Bay
Renfrewshire PA18 6BY

TOP OF THE HILL TRUE BLUES RSC
Mr Robert Swan
21 Robert Street
Port Glasgow
Inverclyde PA14 5RD

2000 TRUE BLUES RSC
Mr John McIntosh
17 Westburn Crescent
Hardgate
Clydebank
Dumbartonshire G81 6PN

THE TAVERN TRUE BLUES
Mr James McClymont
14 Arbuckle Street
Kilmarnock
Ayrshire KA1 3AY

UDDINGSTON NO. 1
Mr K Robertson
4 Laird Grove
Uddingston
Lanarkshire G71

UK LOYAL RSC
Mr Paul Langley
100 Berryknowes Road
Cardonald
Glasgow
Lanarkshire G52 2TT

UNION JACK (BATHGATE) RSC
Mr Steven Gegg
44 Irvine Crescent
Bathgate
West Lothian EH48 2QS

VALE OF LEVEL TEDDY BEARS
Mr Richard McDonald
3 Station Road
Flat 1L
Dumbarton G82 1RY

WATERSIDE RSC
Mr Alan Wishart
30 Blairdenan Avenue
Moodiesburn
Glasgow
Lanarkshire

WELLHOUSE TRUE BLUES RSC
Mr John Money
9b Balado Road
Easterhouse
Glasgow
Lanarkshire G33 4HA

WEST KILBRIDE TRUE BLUES RSC
Mr James Wentworth
1 Drummilling Drive
West Kilbride
Ayrshire KA23 9BE

WESTCOATS RSC
Mr John McNeil
23 Village Road
Cambuslang
Glasgow
Lanarkshire G72 7XD

WESTHILL RSC
Mr Thomas Mcleod
127 Sherry Avenue
Holytown
Motherwell
Lanarkshire ML1 4YE

WESTWOOD RSC
Mr James Gillies
25 Chestnut Crescent
East Kilbride
Glasgow
Lanarkshire G75 9EL

WHIFFLET LOYAL RSC
Mr Andrew Maxwell
139 Dunnottar Avenue
Coatbridge
Lanarkshire ML5 4LP

WHITBURN TRUE BLUES RSC
Mr Edward Dorwood
37 Kirk Brae
Longridge
Bathgate
West Lothian EH47 8AH

WHITEGATES LOYAL RSC
Mr David Mathie
31 Chesters Crescent
Motherwell
Lanarkshire ML1 3QU

WHITEINCH TRUE BLUES RSC
Mr John Massie
41 Kirkoswald Drive
Clydebank
Glasgow
Lanarkshire G81 2DA

WICK & DISTRICT RSC
Mr Ian More
6 Waverley Road
Wick
Caithness KW1 4JA

WILLIE WADDELL NO 1 RSC
Mr George McGregor
c/o Jack Redhouse Cottage
Seafield Road
Bathgate
West Lothian EH47 7AG

WINDSOR RANGERS RSC
Miss Catherine Buchanan
2 Kilmartin Place
Thornliebank
Glasgow
Lanarkshire G46 8DS

WISHAW EAST CROSS RSC
Mr James Whitefield
4 Buchan Street
Coltness
Wishaw
Lanarkshire ML2 7HG

WISHAW CENTRAL RSC
Mr Ronald Walker
9 Redding Road
Strathaven
Lanarkshire ML10 6FA

WEST RENFREWSHIRE RSC
Mr Ronald Steven
8 Devon Drive
Bishopston
Renfrewshire PA7 5EG

QUINTEN YOUNG DRONGAN LOYAL RSC
Mr Sam Kelly
8 Mainsford Avenue
Drongan
Ayr
Ayrshire KA6 7DH

ENGLAND

ABINGDON LOYAL SC
Mr A Jane
52 Appleford Drive
Abingdon
Oxfordshire OX14 2BU

BARROW LOYAL RSC
Mr S paton
4 Delhi Street
Walney Island
Barrow
Cumbria LA14 3BB

BENTINCK RSC
Mr Ian Wandless
6 Newbank Walk
Winlaton
Tyne & Wear NE21 6BQ

BERWICK LOYAL RSC
Mr Colin Gehrman
129 Eastcliffe
Spittal
Berwick-upon-Tweed
Northumberland TD15 2JU

BLACKBURN LOYAL RSC
Mr Ian Gilmour
18 Park Farm Road
Feniscowles
Blackburn
Lancashire BB2 5HW

BLACKPOOL TRUE BLUES
Mr Ray Lennox
16 Dean Street
Blackpool
Lancashire FY4 1AU

BORDER CITY LOYAL RSC
Mr Robert Smith
8 Liddle Close
Lowry Hill
Carlisle
Cumbria CA3 0DP

BRISTOL CHOSEN FEW
Mr Robert Winslow
70 Fremantle House
Dove Street
Kingsdown
Bristol BS2 8LQ

BRIGHTON LOYAL RSC
Mr David Clark
66a Stanmer Park Road
Brighton BN1 7JJ

BASINGSTOKE RSC
Mr B McInally
58 Paterson Close
Kempton Rise
Basingstoke
Hants RG22 4NX

CORBY LOYAL RSC
Mr W M Docherty
152 Shetland Way
Corby
Northamptonshire NN17 2SG

COVENTRY LOYAL
Mr Tony Grimes
129 Mary Slessor Street
Willenhall
Coventry
West Midland CV3 3BE

CHESTER CITY LOYAL RSC
Mr A Speers
133 Garden Lane
Chester
Cheshire CH1 4EY

DARLINGTON TRUE BLUES
Mr R Kennedy
3 Wilson Street
Darlington
County Durham DL3 6QY

EAST DURHAM
Mr Donald Dobell
5 Oswald Terrace
Easington Colliery
Peterlee
County Durham SR8 3LB

ANDY GORAM OLDHAM TRUE BLUES
Mr Marc Turner
27 Chiltern Drive
Royton
Oldham
Lancashire OL2 5TD

GWENT RSC
Mr Andrew Fotheringham
19 Bronllys Place
Croesyceiliog
Cwmbran
Gwent NP44 2DW

HARROWGATE TRUE BLUES
Mr D W Mansfield
4 Borage Road
Killingshall Moor
Harrowgate HG3 2XG

HORWICH LOYAL RSC
Mr M Bridges
17 High Road
Blackrod
Bolton
Lancs BL6 5BP

ISLE OF MAN LOYAL RSC
Mr Ian Gillies
3 Manor Drive
Manor Park
Farmhill
Douglas
Isle of Man IM2 2NX

LEEDS SELECT RSC
Mr R Jackson
338 Selby Road
Whitkirk
Leeds
West Yorkshire LS15 0PR

MILTON KEYNES LOYAL
Mr Alan Paget
56 Field Lane
Greenleys
Milton Keynes
Buckinghamshire MK12 6LP

CHARLIE MILLAR LOYAL
Mr Steve Ramsden
6 Belgrave Road
Oldham
Lancashire OL8 1LS

NEWCASTLETON RSC
Mr James White
Hartsgarth Farm
Nwecastleton
Roxburghshire TD9 0SD

NOTTINGHAM LOYAL RSC
Mr Derek Frazer
37 Norman Road
Newbold
Rugby
Warwickshire CV21 1DP

NORTHAMPTON LOYAL RSC
Mr Alan Whyte
8 Squirrel Chase
Sywell
Northampton NN4 0BD

PLYMOUTH TRUE BLUES RSC
Mr Daniel Forbes
116 Lynher House
Curtis Street
Plymouth
Devon PL1 4HH

PRIDE OF CORBIE RSC
Mr C Smith
82 Highbrook
Corby
Northants NN18 9BA

GRAHAM ROBERTS LOYAL RSC
Mr Andrew Hamilton
68 Cowland Avenue
Enfield
Middlesex EN3 7DH

ROYSTON TRUE BLUES RSC
Mr Peter Yacomine
5 Brampton Road
Royston
Hertfordshire SG8 9TS

SHEFFIELD & DISTRICT LOYAL RSC
Mr Carl Barker
159 Beck lane
Skegby
Sutton-in-Ashfield
Nottinghamshire NG17 3AH

GORDON SMITH LOYAL RSC
Mrs Wendy Damen
70 Lynchet Close
Brighton
East Sussex BN1 7FP

STONEHAVEN LOYAL RSC
Mr James Cowie
9 Shepperton Road
Pettswood
Kent BR5 1DJ

SHETTLESTON SHEILING LOYAL RSC
Mr Robert Lawson
1449 Shettleston Road
Glasgow
Lanarkshire G32 9AT

SUNDERLAND LOYAL RSC
Miss Brenda Galey
30 Pallion Park
Pallion
Sunderland
Tyne & Wear SR4 6QE

SKELMERSDALE ORANGE & BLUE RSC
Mr Dennis Rawsthorne
210 Yewdale
Westbank
Skelmersdale
Lancashire WN8 6ER

STOCKPORT TRUE BLUES RSC
Mr Garry Irvin
10 Meerbrook Road
Cheadle Heath
Stockport
Cheshire SU3 0NJ

SOUTHAMPTON RSC
Mr Alan Fraser
80 Stafford Road
Shirley
Southampton SO15 5ED

TIPTREE RSC
Miss Lynn Anderson
10 Walnut Tree Way
Tiptree
Colchester
Essex CO5 0NG

WOKING RSC
Mr David MacNeill
Security Flight
RAF Oakhanger
Bordon
Hampshire GU35 9HU

WESTCOUNTRY LOYAL RSC
Mr Lance Higgins
6 Railton Jones Close
Stoke Gifford
Bristol BS34 8BF

ABROAD

ADELAIDE RSC
Mr Charles Morrison
14 Adrian Street
Christie Downs
Adelaide
Australia 5164

AJAX PICKERING RSC
Ms Maggie Houston
10 Thorncroft Crescent
AJAX
Ontario
Canada L15 2S2

JORG ALBERTZ LOYAL NUREMBERG RSC
Mr Gary Mackay
Untere Kramers Gasse 18
Nuremberg
Germany 90403

BANGKOK RSC
Mr David Murray
#601 P.Phan Mansion
67/3 Soi Saengchan
Bangkok
Thailand 10110

BOSTON RSC
Mr Arthue McIntyre
472 Centre Street
Pembroke
Massachusetts
USA 02339

CANADIAN WINDSOR RSC
Mr John Campbell
236 Fairway Crescent
St Clair Beach
Ontario
Canada NN8N 2Z2

DETROIT WINDSOR RSC
Mr Thomas Plunkett
8151 Clay court
Sterling Heights
Michigan
USA 48313

FLORIDA RSC
Mr David Robertson
6755 Miami Lakes Drive
Apt J136
Miami Lakes
Florida 33014

IBROX EXILES
Mr John Stewart
1 Belleau Street
Stoney Creek
Ontario
Canada L8J 1N1

JOHANNESBURG RANGERS
Mr Graham Gersbach
P O Box 965
Edenvale
Gauteng
South Africa 1610

KEARNY NEW JERSEY
Mr Leslie White
127 William Street
Kearny
New Jersey
USA 07032

LONDON ONTARIO
Mr David Fife
51 Mendip Crescent
London
Ontario
Canada N6E 1H2

MELBOURNE RSC
Mr Ray Newall
1 Northgate Way
Langwarrin
Victoria
Australia 3910

MICHAEL MOLS UTRECHT RSC
Mr George Duncan
Steinenburghlaan 1
Debilt
Utrecht
Holland 3731 GG

NEW SOUTH WALES RSC
Mr James McLeigh
25 MacIntyre Crescent
Ruse
New South Wales
Australia 2560

ORANGE COUNTY RSC
Ms Gayla Stewart
8118 Chicopec Avenue
Northridge
California
USA 91325

PARIS RANGERS LOYAL
Mr James Reid
36 Rue Trebois
Levallois-Perret
Paris
France 92300

ROOTY HILL RSC NEW SOUTH WALES
Mr Alexander Sancroft
44 Radburn Road
Hebersham
New South Wales 2770

SYDNEY RSC
Mr Andrew Gill
45 Rose Street
Chippendale
New South Wales 2008

SINGAPORE DAVIE COOPER MEMORIAL RSC
Mr William McAdam
3 Holland Park
#02-03 Hollandswood Court
Singapore 249473

TASMANIAN RSC
Mr Andy Baxter
37 Banjorrah Street
Howray
Tasmania
Australia 7018

TORONTO CENTRAL RSC
Mr Todd Van Allen
124 Medland Street
Toronto
Canada M6P ZN5

VANCOUVER BRANCH 2 RSC
Mr David Fletcher
700 Delestre Avenue
Coquitlam
British Columbia V3K 2E9

WINNIPEG RSC
Mr David Simpson
398 Centennial Street
Winnipeg
Canada R3N 1P5

WASHINGTON DC LOYAL RSC
Mr Richard Hamilton
c/o British Embassy
Washington DC
USA PFP02

The Fans: The team thank the Ibrox faithful for their support over the season.